The Rabbit
Between
Us

Im Zug
Michael Sowa

VICTOR MENZA

The Rabbit
Between
Us

LONDON NEW YORK CALCUTTA

Seagull Books, 2021

Victor Menza, *The Rabbit Between Us*
© Lynn Zorn, 2021

ISBN   978 0 8574 2 797 7

British Library Cataloguing-in-Publication Data
A catalogue record for this book is available from the British Library.

Typeset by Seagull Books, Calcutta, India
Printed and bound by Versa Press, East Peoria, Illinois, USA

CONTENTS

1

CHAPTER I

Psychic Bolt-Holes

24

CHAPTER II

Visitation

41

CHAPTER III

I Never Saw *Harvey*

50

CHAPTER IV

What Is a Symbol

59

CHAPTER V

Down the Philosophical Rabbit-Hole
or "GAVAGAI!"

68

CHAPTER VI

The Rabbit Evangels:
Joel Chandler Harris and Beatrix Potter

97

CHAPTER VII

Obliterature

114

CHAPTER VIII

How Children Get Cheated Out of Their Humanity

130

CHAPTER IX

The Rabbit Between Us Came from Slavery

145

CHAPTER X

Aubade with Brer Rabbit

157

CHAPTER XI

The Rabbit Dances

163

Notes

183

List of Illustrations

I

PSYCHIC BOLT-HOLES

We want to say: "When we mean something, it's like going up to someone, it's not having a dead picture (of any kind)." We go up to the thing we mean.

—Wittgenstein, *Philosophical Investigations*

You left me two summers ago with a lovely note on a postcard of one of Sowa's animal paintings—*Im Zug*—showing a rabbit seated alone in a railway compartment. The rabbit, wearing a nice jacket, looks obedient and abandoned and must be young because its legs do not even reach the edge of the seat. From the mood of the picture, especially the view out the window of clouds stretching over close-set houses and waning sunlight coming low from the left, the train is clearly *leaving*. Arrivals just do not feel like this. And it's moving slowly because nothing outside the window is blurred. I also felt pretty certain that the rabbit, sitting so primly in the middle of the upholstered benchseat, is pulling away from us, its back to the engine, and that the dynamics of the picture works like this:

This arrow is the first of two tributes to Fletcher Rabbit,
who delivered the mail on *Kukla, Fran, and Ollie.*

I obtained the book from which the picture came, and found out the rabbit's name is Esterhazy; he's on his way to Berlin, and his parents and countless relatives are all weeping on the platform.

In the wake of your leaving, two little mysteries about the postcard began to shape up for me. The first you engaged straight off in your note: "Even I figured out what this bunny was saying—doing—up to. But it's too sad for me to think about, or write about right now." I understand the unlikeliness of *you* figuring out what the bunny was up to ("Even I . . .") not to be due to any lack of yours as an interpreter, because you had to interrupt the quiet upsurge (there were tears behind it) that led you to choose the card and inscribe it with so many angel words of love and goodbye. Toward the end of your note, you actually brushed—surely unconsciously—right up against the first little mystery. A dozen or so words that began (appropriately enough) "I hate visitation . . . ," out came the phrase ". . . feeling like I'm becoming somebody else," followed by a dash (—).

So the little rabbit on the train was *you*. But what is so mysterious about that? Given the circumstance of your leaving, obviously the bunny stood for you, and without anybody needing to say it. In fact the identity between you and the bunny was felt all the stronger for not being stated. Mentioning it would have exposed it to various forms of being pulled apart. Any comment would have been the beginning of an obstructed view, would likely have invested the picture with its own contingencies; grabbing the silence by a particular set of ears and talking about them as if there weren't a whole creature suspended below. On the day you left, none of us—not you, not me, not Lynn—said *anything* about the content of the picture, though (because) we were all moved by it. An image of a rabbit standing for a person may be a routine sort of thing, but in this instance, it unquestionably gathered about itself a protective silence.

Gregor Samsa awakens one morning to find himself transformed into a giant insect. What happens to him, his treatment by his family, his supervisor, etc., is appalling and poignant. *The Metamorphosis* is a serious, troubling story; it lodges in us the way the apple lodges in Gregor's back. On the morning of your departure, you produced a card depicting (you as) a little rabbit leaving on a train; a card which you furtively acquired the day before at Bear Pond Books in Montpelier, a card which pretty much struck me the way the queen of diamonds struck when Angela Lansbury flashes it in *The Manchurian Candidate*. So in our story—a sad one—someone (you) tacitly but really asserts that she has been fictionally turned into a rabbit. In Kafka's story, the narrator fictionally asserts that someone has really turned into a cockroach.

Which transformation is more serious?

By the next afternoon, having already heard from you that you had arrived home safely on the opposite side of the country, the little representational mystery of yesterday had grown into a full-fledged paradox. The normal separation between a representation and whatever it represents ("signifier"/"signified") was not working for me. Lying on my desk, the postcard had become a locus where one could visit you and be in your presence. And this without any illusion of seeing you or imagining your voice. The postcard, of course, was not a *likeness* of you, although it was very much *of* you and in that sense extremely *like* you. Nor was it a relic—a lock of hair, a piece of clothing—because it was nothing detached or removed from you. Anyway, relics and mementos tend to make me sad, make me miss whomever they are of. But the Sowa picture, as I say, without the least looking like you, was having the contrary effect—it was making me miss you less, it was seeming to establish some sort of contact with you *in propria persona*. What was going on?

The most sacred image on the Athenian Acropolis was that of the goddess Athena Polias, the guardian of the city. It was an idol made of olivewood and of such antiquity that no one knew for sure where it came from. The soldiers who were left to defend the Acropolis against the attack of the Persians felt an acute sense of abandonment when the totem was removed to the offshore island of Salamis for safekeeping. According to the Christian

Tertullian, examining the statue many centuries later, the almighty object was nothing more than "a rough stake and a shapeless piece of wood." And that is how it was with these (to use the technical Greek term) *xoana*. They were barely worked wooden planks, summarily carved with minimal indications of limbs and eyes. Porphyry observed of such statues that the more refined ("illusionistic") they were, the less divine. If we take that with the fact that the origins of any *xoanon* were generally uncertain (like the black meteoric stones that were also objects of cult worship, *xoana* were often thought to fall from heaven), it seems that the power of these images to contain, to *be*, some divinity, has everything to do with their coming from outside human devising (human *mechanē*) but landing miraculously inside the circle of human meaning. I think this is why Pausanias described such statues as "strange" (*atopos, xenos*).

We are very close here to the formula, as I understand it, for the uncanny: an outside without the proper insides or an inside without the proper outsides.

Even though you presented it in a perfectly normal manner— no flourishes, no evidence of sleight-of-hand—the postcard seemed to materialize out of nowhere, and startlingly so. Maybe this was because no sooner did I see it than the sense of it overwhelmed me; and that is perhaps just a roundabout way of saying that the rabbit jumped right out at me and set me to trembling.

Of course my reaction was not completely inexplicable. I really had no idea where you had come up with it. But much more than that, I could not believe that such a postcard existed. Way beyond "appropriate," it had the force of an impossible coincidence. You had introduced me to Sowa years ago, and he won a good piece of my heart when I saw what I took to be a serious painting of his showing a group of potatoes marching through a town. (This was before I learned what lay behind my father's oft-repeated remark about my origins: "We found you in a potato patch." This set up a riddling internal connection between me and potatoes, one that drove me to distraction when reading Machado de Assis's novel about a philosopher—*Quincas Borba*—with the motto "To the victor, the potatoes.") All this added to the coincidence. But the coincidence itself consisted in the near-perfect correspondence between the situation in the postcard (the bunny about to disappear) and the situation simultaneously visible on the very same axis in the window standing directly behind the postcard—the road on which you were shortly to be leaving and the bend around which you would disappear, a road which has always reminded me of the soft tree-lined lanes that climb the northern neighborhoods of Tehran (which, of course, I have only seen in movies). An allegory may twinkle, but it is not supposed to be able to unfold like this before your eyes. The circumstance of a *xoanon*, where and how it showed up, had everything to do with its force and perpetuation. Just so, there was a reverberant ring of circumstances around the little postcard.

The wooden idols that Pausanias saw were not only dense with legend and circumstance, they were also roughed out in what was called a pillar-shape—a very resonant form for the Greeks. The kind of wood (i.e. olivewood) was also very significant. A *xoanon* did not, therefore, radiate from an empty center. The statue was, after all, divine, and it had to be suitable for authentic contact with a god.

And that brings me to the second little mystery of the postcard. At its apparitional center sits a bunny with the same expression of abstracted stillness worn by rabbits stopped in the wild, eyes always seeming to be angled off from your own. How did this kind of creature become such a powerful way of feeling your presence? *What do rabbits mean?* Everything that I have been trying to describe above as happening so mysteriously and so suddenly, happened pictorially, without the aid of words. Your note on the back of the card was like a separate event—behind the main show. In this country—with the prominent exception of Bugs Bunny—rabbits tacitly evoke all the sentiments that go into humanity and the repressed memory of the sin of slavery. This is enough to establish a profound connection between the Brer Rabbit stories and Jesus Christ—something we shall explore in detail later on. As you know, rabbits of one kind or other have figured in our life together from early on, and this is not to count the role of the Easter Bunny that your mother for obvious reasons (her Scarlett O'Hara penchant) assigned to my household. The Easter Bunny was a rumor, a phantom; I mean we never *saw* him—the baskets were full, but the tomb was empty (*Christus anesti*). Of the rabbits that actually showed up for us, I remember:

(a) *Brown Bunny*: Whom you too will surely remember from your sister Margie's ever-increasing detachment of stuffed animals and other transitional objects (Shell was a pillow and Pinky a blanket) that she slept with one by one in an order as rigorous and unbending as our visitation schedule. I am not sure where in the rotation Brown Bunny's turn came. I think it must have been toward the beginning, since he was—as those suspiciously *sui generis* Vermonters refer to themselves—an "original." I was especially fond of him with his cartoony happy-to-see-you-let's-play! demeanor. Without knowing exactly why, I used to root for his turn to fall within visitation, and always felt a tiny elation when he'd pop out of the overnight bag. It eventually transpired that my favoritism here was that of straight-ahead identification. Through the magic of forgetting his origins, I had made the same mystery out of his life that amnesia had made out of mine. Just as I had belonged to someone else—my biological mother—Brown Bunny had been *my* stuffed animal. He was given to me in 1977 by a woman who had a pretty good picture of my needs. He was assigned the job of night-watchman on my bedside table. His little arms were extended, ready for a hug, like the Cristo Redentor on Corcovado. Margie first eye-balled him when I brought the two of you down to Baltimore for a visit in the summer of 1978. He wound up going back to New England as a souvenir in Margie's possession and achieved a place for himself in her apostolic zoo. I wonder where he is today.

(b) *Cottontails on Cape Cod*: All you had to do was look and there they were, two or three of them paused at various spots around the lawn. Since rabbits like people are averse to being studied on, they were doing their version of freeze-frame, blending into the background. We could imagine that they were inviting us to some form of croquet or a game of connect-the-bunnies. Throughout the summer they turned up like abundant little accent pieces that kept all of us in open spirits. The two great Augusts that we spent in the cottage off Coast Guard Beach were really the first time that we came into our own, where we could relax and open out into the outdoors. Unlike the Upper Connecticut River Valley (where we lived), we never ran into anyone judging the accidentality of our family. For weeks on end we were never *late* for anything. We read *Sylvie and Bruno* (where we learned the danger of being too sober; since while a drunk sees one thing as two, an excessively sober individual sees two things as one). We proved that the book could even be read outdoors at midnight by the light of the moon. We learned about greenheads, rosehips, skatepurses, sand dollars, terns, hummocks, spring tides, and that when we were in the water, there was nothing between us and Portugal (so be careful). About marshgrass, alewives, tryworks, and runnels. Lyme disease had not made it from the germ-warfare lab on Plum Island to Cape Cod back then, so we could hike in the woods without fear. Of all this, the replacement of fear and self-consciousness with curiosity and gentleness, the rabbits were the emblem and keepers of it. "There's one!" "There goes another!"

(c) *Blue Bunnies*: One Halloween, I think around the time of the Cape Cod years, Lynn and I got you up as matching bunnies. You each wore furry blue jumpsuit-style pajamas—like sleepers for big kids. The rabbitness of the costume came down to essentials: big white ears attached to a headband that tied at the nape of your neck and a white pom-pom pinned to your backside. Since we did not really live in a neighborhood, we had to drive up to town so you could go trick-or-treating and really get to be bunnies. We parked at the head of a street where you thought the pickings would be good. Lynn and I were to wait in the car while you and Margie worked your way down the block. I do not recall there being any streetlamps, and the house windows and scattered porch lights seemed to keep their illumination to themselves. Just a few houses down from the car the main swath of the street seemed to lay in total blackness—and it was not long before you and Margie entered it. I started to panic as soon as I realized that I would not be able to keep track of you as you went from house to house. This special occasion seemed to have fallen into an abyss. But then a wonderful thing happened. As we got adjusted to looking into the dark, we could make out your white puffball tails, making bouncy curlicues back and forth across the street, disappearing behind a hedge or onto a porch and then rematerializing in the opposite direction. The pom-poms were not made of any special glow-in-the-dark fabric, but from plain white cotton. I guess I should not have been surprised at their visibility in such darkness and at that distance ("wear white at night" was a current maxim). But surprised and delighted I was. For me, being able to follow those two little synecdoches in the dark was a demonstration on the order of something that happened when we were sitting on the beach at Cape Cod in the pitch-dark and the only thing we could see was the phosphorescent ribbon on the surf. How two pom-poms managed to gather so much light out of the black New England air seemed no less miraculous. This episode put me in mind of a beautiful image to which Pirandello likened the moment of his birth. "One night in June I dropped down like a firefly beneath a huge pine tree standing all on its own in an olive grove on the edge of a blue clay plateau overlooking the African Sea. We know about fireflies. It's as if the blackness of night exists solely for their benefit, so that, as they fly this way and that, they can show off their pale green gleam. Every now and then one of them falls and, on the ground, gives a sigh of green light as if from very far away. That was how I dropped down on that June night . . ." Even though I am no longer half-Italian (I now prefer to think of myself as half-Phoenician), this image is followed in my mind by the Vermont-born slander that Italian stoneworkers in Barre used to eat fat robins. I also take umbrage at Vermonters calling poplars (in their dialect, *popples*) a "trash tree," since a pretty part of my youth was spent watching poplars shimmer in the wind.

(d) *White Rabbit in the Snow* (Rabbit Inferred?): In 1994, for the first time, Lynn and I attempted to skip out on winter in New England, a winter that turned out to be the most severe in our lifetime. We left Vermont in a blizzard that reached all the way down to the Eastern Shore of Virginia. The next day in North Carolina we encountered lows of two degrees below zero. The winter-zone never really broke until South Florida, where we finally hit temperatures in the eighties. Having set up in Key West, we were now 1500 miles from you finishing up your last term of college back in Vermont and soon to start work as an ICU nurse at Fletcher Allen Hospital. Come February I had the first inkling of a feeling that began to set in each year with increasing tenacity around your birthday, a feeling that I later described as that of being "flummoxed"—prevented from the ecstasy of coming out of myself to embrace you on the anniversary of meeting my first blood relative. I fought the flummox off by writing a birthday poem to you, starring a white rabbit (probably a snowshoe hare) who was to carry my birthday wish for you north. He was invisible but for a "crystal rooster plume" made by his ears as he pushed furiously through the snow that was over his head. That was really all I had to give you on your birthday: an image of something you could not see. The distances between us were becoming impossible, so the rabbit had to bear the burden of invisibility. I made him white to ensure that you would not think you saw him even if his head occasionally bobbed above the snowline. The painter Robert Ryman made monochrome paintings out of white, having discovered that it was the best color for making other, nonchromatic aspects of the painting visible. *White surfaces are excellent for reading into.* So love was thinned out to thoughts and their conveyance.

I should confess to a built-in inaccuracy. I sent the poem to you in Burlington, but the situation of the image as I secretly pictured it was of the rabbit coming down off Sawnee Bean Road and tearing into the dooryard of your mother's former house in Thetford where you were waiting at the window. A hundred miles away. North then. But how now, given that you've spent your last five birthdays in New Zealand? I would need a much tougher rabbit to swim and scamper along the great curves of the earth; that would be the swamp rabbit named Riley. As they say at the dog races, "Here comes the rabbit!"

(e) *The Deictic (Pointing) Bunny*: By the year 2000, you had clearly caught the spirit of my *cartes de non visite* and arranged from California to have a Victoria Blewer photograph sent to me in Vermont for my birthday. It shows an old chipping wooden billboard with a large rabbit silhouette on it next to the words "HERE IT IS" painted in big block letters. The profile is of a rabbit sitting not straight up on its hind legs, but rather tilted forward, front paws on the ground in the "get set" position. (You might say, if you were willing to add an "r" to one of the

canonical attitudes for sculptured lions, that the rabbit is *crouchant*.) I had seen this kind of rabbit before along roadsides in our travels through the South. And to tell the truth, it seems like natural work for rabbits, or rather their pictographic off-spring, to help with matters of attention. Without the rabbit next to it, the sentence "HERE IT IS" would be left with its near-empty clamoring about some "here" (where?), some "it" (what?), and some "is" (now?) to verge on a private hysteria. But the rabbit, again working *solely through the eye,* keeps everything calm and quiet by absorbing all these deictic anxieties into its rabbit form. You might say it strokes us before the crazy owners of the sign start talking. A rabbit seen at rest (as opposed to in motion) is for us a natural, pure, and therefore precious declaration of a something here and now. It is almost as if it had been assigned this indexical role in some animal grammar—back when our principal communication was through dancing—the meaning of which we have mostly lost. It was a compromise of this power that led Alice down the rabbit-hole. There was nothing so very remarkable about a white rabbit with pink eyes that ran close by her; nor anything so very much out of the way when Alice understood the rabbit to say to itself, "Oh dear! Oh dear! I shall be too late!" But what made her jump to her feet was the rabbit's taking a watch out of its waistcoat pocket and looking at it. A rabbit enslaved to conventional time—that was something to get curious about. The very lord of deixis enfeoffed!

The billboard itself sits in the middle of a very American nowhere, a parched, scrubby stretch of what looks like West Texas desert. Everything in the picture—except for the sign and a cluster of maybe farm buildings behind it a few hundred yards down the road—seems to be running out to the horizon. On the right, an empty two-lane blacktop; on the left, a railroad embankment, and all manner of poles and posts stringing power lines and barbed wire in roughly the same direction (dare I say it: West). Whatever HERE there used to be at the sign is obviously over and gone. Little jigsawed animals on the top of the sign—some of them broken off—suggest that the site used to be something attractive to children, something lighthearted. At first the picture looks to be black-and-white, but it slowly dawns on one that the billboard is definitely yellow, after which perceptible green and straw colors can be seen in the scrub; and for the rest—sky, ground, poles, and wires—sepia just might be the visual truth, leaving us with the final ambiguity: the color of the rabbit and the lettering. Here we can almost see, but are ultimately forced to conjecture (i.e. feel), that they are colored red.

So far as the photo goes, the billboard is like a yellow band-aid placed over what would be its vanishing point, which from all indications lies in the same quarter as the wound of Manifest Destiny.

Of course the picture is a kind of joke, the punchline of which was delivered much earlier by Gertrude Stein when she wrote of her childhood home—you recently absquatulated to a town nearby—that "there is no there there." It was in that spirit (gently reinforced by the fact that the photographer was from Vermont) that I understood the picture as a token of your promise that your move was not permanent. I began to wonder what Stein's thought might mean if applied to time. A place where there is no "there there" could be distressing, even desolate. But a time when there is no "now now" is positively funereal.

(f) *Turner's* Rain, Steam, and a Hare: Soon after I started writing about Sowa's *Im Zug,* I remembered another painting involving a hare and a train (of which I have a postcard reproduction that I now keep with your postcard in a folder, along with my notes for this letter). The painting depicts a locomotive barreling from the center of the landscape just as it is crossing onto the Maidenhead Bridge over the Thames, heading for the lower right corner. The engine looks like an open, roaring furnace that is starting to burn a hole in the center of the painting. On the tracks out in front of the train is a hare running for its life. Turner thought enough of this hare to point it out to a young boy who happened to be watching him—nose nearly touching the canvas—as he worked. It needed pointing out, because while it is assuredly there, it is painted so lightly, so minimally (I think of him as having done it with his fingernail), that one can miss

it. In fact in many current reproductions, including my postcard, it simply does not turn up. A few months ago I spent a good hour ruining my eyes as I scrutinized every color plate I had of the painting, even using a magnifying glass, hoping for a rabbit aspect to dawn in the paint. My failure to find it sank into me like a lug nut of anxiety that stayed with me until I finally found a good reproduction at the bookstore a few days later. There was the hare bounding down the tracks—no squinting, no special optics necessary. Even now, though, I get a little nervous asserting its existence when I cannot simply turn and take a look at it. I am thankful for all the recorded references to it, Turner's own most of all. One recent commentator, after describing the animal's predicament, asked why it doesn't jump aside and save its life. I can imagine Turner replying, "It's a hare! A hare thinks to outrun danger on the ground." That is the tragedy of the picture.

Eventually I could see why I felt *Im Zug* and *Rain, Steam, and Speed* (the correct name) belonged together. Sowa's painting, obviously without intending it, is an amazing top-to-bottom inversion of Turner's. The wide exterior space of the latter has become the upright internal space of the former. Turner's hare runs from imminent death toward the lower right corner:

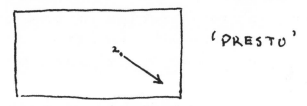

Second tribute to Fletcher Rabbit.

Sowa's bunny sits safely and from an almost exactly corresponding spot recedes slowly to the upper right corner. The situation in the well-lit real space of Turner's painting has been driven via slavery (Brer Rabbit) and Victorian childhood (Peter Rabbit) to the shadowy fantasy space of Sowa's painting where we live now. Between the two pictures we can trace what has become of the rabbit symbol.

The same thing that bore down on the English countryside in 1844 bore down on us in Vermont and our rabbits. Even back then it was no mere locomotive, but an ever-more universal and relentless technological intention—a kind of cult that looks to an outsider like the Cult of the Unforeseeable Effect or the Cult of Get Out of the Way. As the reforestation of Vermont got underway in the last quarter of the nineteenth century, porcupines became a "serious problem" to the "wood-based economy" of the state, since they like to eat their way through the bark of what happened to be valuable timber trees. In 1959 the Vermont Department of Forestry and Parks, in concert with the Vermont Fish and Wildlife Department and the U.S. Fish and Wildlife Service, began a "program" to "combat" the porcupine problem. Over a period of eight years, 124 "fisher-cats" live-trapped in Maine were brought into the state. The fisher (not a cat but a black weasel) is a very efficient night hunter, and one of the few natural predators agile and quick enough to knock a porcupine out of a tree and attack its belly without getting quilled. According to the guidebook from which the above-quoted language comes, the fisher has been "endowed with an aura of ferocity and evil." The author refers derisively to stories of fishers "carrying off dogs, cattle, and even children," and concludes that the "program has worked well," that fishers have "proved a significant control on the porcupines," and that the trappers' results will enable wildlife biologists to "gain insights into the population dynamics of this exciting 'black ghost' of the forest." I have not heard anyone talk about the abduction of dogs or cows, but I do know a father who had to rescue his child from a snarling fisher at the back door of their house. More to the point, while the program may have been a cheap and effective way to restrain porcupines, it pretty much eliminated the rabbit population of the state and made it a very bad idea to let your domestic cat out at night.

—Oh, by the way, "hare" is also a British slang word for a passenger traveling without a ticket.

(g) *Second Thoughts about My Two Buckteeth and Rabbit's Foot*: Looking back at my youth and childhood, I believe I can now see a root or two of a predisposition in the matter of rabbits, in particular how someone who saw into me gave me Brown Bunny to pull guard-duty on my nightstand during the most dire stretch of my life. It's hard to say where rabbithood first sank into me, but I strongly suspect it was over the phenomenon of buckteeth. I had two big ones which earned me the nickname Bugs Bunny from my father. "Look, Olive, it's Bugs!" I liked Bugs Bunny, but not the nickname. I also remember feeling very bad for a boy in my neighborhood who had what was called a "hare lip." In fact my father's little bit of mockery isolated me more than I understood, because I could plainly see that neither of my parents' teeth were remotely like my own (just as you can see that Margie has her mother's front teeth and you have mine). I think I have just discovered the source of my affection for Bugs Bunny's impertinent tagline (which, given that my father was a doctor, I always heard as delightfully disrespectful), "What's up, Doc?"

Next comes an item I cannot quite make my peace with. For the better part of my boyhood up to adolescence, I carried a rabbit's foot, a real rabbit's foot with brown and white fur and sharp phalanges. I loved it, loved the feel of it, a so-called good luck charm. If asked why I carried it, I probably would have said for "good luck." But for the life of me I do not think that at that age "luck"—good or bad—was much of a concept for me; and it never would have occurred to me to try to manipulate fortune. I felt like rolled dice. Although it would have embarrassed me to say it, what I really derived from the rabbit's foot was *comfort*. (I could not have said it because I could not have explained it. It was tied to the secret of my adoption.) Less strange, but strange nonetheless, was that I never made a mental connection between the rabbit's foot and a formerly living rabbit. Not once, and this despite believing that it was real and being well aware of its creaturely attributes—the fur, the toenails, and the little bones you could shift a bit. When I learned a few things recently about the history of the rabbit's foot, I began to wonder if the meaning of the odd object wasn't laid right up in the object itself, so that hearing just the minimum a child might grasp its magical significance. The principal use of the rabbit's foot is not to secure good things but to avert bad—"apotropaic," as they say in the trade—and not just any old bad things but primarily ghosts. I first learned of this from an anecdote about John B. Watson, founding father of American psychological behaviorism. A Southerner, Watson once confessed to a fear of ghosts dating from childhood that was so strong that even as a grown man he could not be paid to go into a graveyard at night, even if he had in his pocket the left hind foot of a rabbit shot at midnight during the dark of the moon. Like Watson, I had ghost troubles too, but they were—because of their content—unavowable. I was reduced at my residential tryworks to a generalized fear of the dark (*pavor nocturnus*) which had ineffable offspring in the daytime. It was with the latter, little phobic spots during the day, that the rabbit's foot came in handy without my ever realizing it. In retrospect it seems to have functioned for me as a Freudian fetish object. My attention confined itself obediently and strictly to the *detached object,* keeping clear of any thought of the lost main body. I would grab hold of it the way a baby grabs hold of your finger. I know it's asymmetrical, but that remains for me the warmest way to hold someone's hand. I would have to dismiss all of this as a private elaboration on the use of a rabbit's foot to deal with the ghost of my biological mother who was expelled from the Catholic home for unwed mothers when I was six weeks old. Like other rabbit's feet, the particular one I had must have derived from a *shape-shifted witch*.

My nightfears were focused on the eyes of a portrait of the Blessed Virgin Mary holding the baby Jesus, which my parents hung in my room across from my headboard. This opened up an unconscious tunnel to the bedroom of the woman who saved my life, my adoptive Italian grandmother, Amelia, who had a shrine on her dressing table to the Blessed Virgin, which was always accompanied by a lit votive candle in a red glass. My grandmother carried me on her hip and fed me goat's milk and pigeon soup for a total of six months. My adoptive parents said it was two weeks. They lied.

(h) *Excursus on Porch Rabbits*: Growing up as I did in the city, I do not recall ever seeing a rabbit in the wild (i.e. a "Rabbit!"). I did see live rabbits, however, when I was in grammar school, thanks to a short-lived craze for pet white rabbits. I remember having my own pet rabbit ever so briefly, in a box in our back hall for a few days, arriving and quickly departing under mysterious circumstances. What I remember is that in one home after another, these "pets" were kept in open boxes covered either with a screen or chicken wire, usually on the back porch. Thus began an eerie association of the domestic limbo of the porch (*attached* to the house but not *in* it) with hard times for rabbits. They always seemed miserable and tended toward sickly in their cages. This thought was next compounded in high school when my friend of the time, Vinny DiMarco, started complaining about the hullaballoo around his house caused by his step-mother's having undertaken to make *hasenpfeffer* (peppered rabbit stew), which meant, among other things, giving over the front porch to pickling the rabbit meat in vinegar and spices. I think what bothered Vinny was all the high drama of "Coming soon! Hasenpfeffer!" On the third or fourth day of pickling, I dropped by and indeed there it was on the far side of the porch. I never heard how it tasted. (I should note that for me eating rabbit is taboo.)

My last encounter with a real rabbit before coming to New England happened in college, and once again on a porch. A friend of mine, a graduate student in English and a great admirer of Hemingway's hunting stories, shot a rabbit in the hills southeast of Buffalo and left it hanging on the porch of the house which he rented with two other students while he went home to Los Angeles for the Christmas break. The weather, which had been of the chilly, late fall variety, suddenly turned to full-bore winter with snow and very cold temperatures. Soon the rabbit was frozen stiff. Stretched out along the railing in a permanent bounding position with snow crystals and ice in its fur, it began to bother the landlady and his roommates as well. There was talk of throwing it out, since no one wanted to look at it for another three weeks (when classes would resume and little Hemingway would be back). The freezing temperatures were holding pretty steady, so I decided to wrap the rabbit up and mail it to California. What in the name of Fletcher Rabbit was I thinking! Having been sent parcel post, the rabbit thawed out while sitting in the Elmwood Avenue post office and raised a big stink. It was returned in the box right back to the porch, whereupon Mrs. Catalano—the landlady—promptly dispatched it. This was the third time in my life (only one of them deliberate) that I emerged as a prankster with the postal system. At age five, Jo Ostendorf and I, imitating what we saw our fathers do every night and thinking we were performing a public service, went door to door down our block ripping up mail in the mailman's wake. Seven years later in an inexcusably adolescent frame of mind, I put a good-sized live cat into the U.S. Mail box at the corner of Lafayette Avenue and Gates Circle, and went home to imagine how the next mail pickup would go. I apologize.

So much for the fey category of porch rabbit. A porch is a tremulous place.

II

VISITATION

"Ah, your favorites are among these!" I continued,
turning to an obscure cushion full of something like cats.
"A strange choice of favorites," she observed scornfully.
Unluckily, it was a heap of dead rabbits.
—Lockwood, attempting to have a pleasant visit at
Wuthering Heights

When I became a noncustodial father in January of 1976, all of
our visitation for the next eighteen years was via a Rabbit—
a Volkswagen Rabbit—the first one for seven years and the
second one for eleven more. So every visit began and ended
inside a Rabbit. Does that mean that the rabbit between us stood
for a car and not an animal? Absolutely not, because spirit col-
lects around a name. That is why *nomen est omen*. When it
comes to choosing a car, I have never been much possessed by
automotive rationality. My first car, a Triumph, was a play on my
name. I proceed more in the manner in which I buy clothes. Can
I see myself in this car? Is it me? (Maybe I am guilty of hearing
into the etymology of "automotive"—"self-motives.") Cars are

expressive, and any form of expression must have more than one outlet. This points to the weakness in the Latin proverb that about matters of taste there can be no disputing (*de gustibus disputandum est*). If you are lucky and hit on the source of the taste, the pleasure in it may collapse. This thought deteriorated in English into a lazy falsehood which helps people avoid knowing one another: "There's no accounting for taste." It is espoused by the nasty aunt, Madame Cheron, in *The Mysteries of Udolpho,* who cares not a whit about her niece's insides.

Looking back on it from this distance (thirty-eight years), I would have to say that more than a routine matter of self-expression, my choice of a Rabbit was positively demonic; that I was going to have to be transformed in order to survive. I was letting a new allegory loose in my life. I could hardly have acted in a less utilitarian manner. About the car itself I knew only that it had front-wheel drive, so I could imagine it handling the unplowed or steep stretches of backroad where Lynn and I were going to have to find places to live. I understood also that it was supposed to get good gas mileage, which along with the price tag fit with the fact that we had very little money. I talked all this up endlessly to my father who was going to have to pay for the car, but it was nothing more than a cover story for my direct desire to be driving a Rabbit. There were other cars that were less expensive, performed well in the snow, got better mileage, and were less costly to maintain. I did no "research" whatsoever on the Rabbit. I talked only to salespeople, not to any current or past owners, and road-tested the particular one I bought (whose color was a garish yellow) with a two-minute drive around the block. I left Buffalo in possession of a car that turned out to be chronically difficult (often impossible) to start in cold weather. The heater was weak and sometimes did not work at all. The electrical system was incurably palsied, and the car never got anywhere near its advertised miles per gallon. By its seventh year I could see clear to the road through holes in the floor in front of the driver's seat. My response? I went out and bought another Rabbit (with a different but equally displeasing color).

I definitely seem to have been in the grip of some kind of cosmic engagement with the idea of a rabbit. In buying an uppercase Rabbit, I hoped to open up a relation to the real lowercase rabbit, a relation—to admit the full insanity of it—that I might climb inside of like Osiris into a hare. What did I have in mind? Something of an answer can be had from the circumstances I returned to after your mother and I separated in Edinburgh, Scotland. I had been forced into the Wilderness of Divorce where I felt as if I would be devoured. A big dispossession was underway: I was to lose my share of the house and all the moveable property therein, but for my books and a trunk of clothes; three-quarters of my paycheck was being attached; and my credit rating was on the brink of ruin and soon went over it. All of our so-called friends had denounced me, and people who used to be happy to see me now turned away at my approach. My mother and father were in receipt of a series of hyperbolic letters from your mother describing my role in the breakup of our marriage (leaving out her affair of two and a half years that ended another marriage) and the overstated "destitution" I had left you in. Even worse, the backroom whispering that eventually would cost me my job and my future in the academy had already started. Clearly your mother and her allies had outmaneuvered me (not that hard to do), and I was to become, as often happens in divorce, the excommunicated party. It makes things easier for everyone else—except the children. I found all of this very frightening. And it stayed frightening. The fact that I had always felt myself to be something of an outsider only increased my dread at having now to live as one. In truth, the three or four people who could directly affect my standing in the community were looking to drive me out altogether. (But not President John Kemeny, who knew that I functioned like a cheap Student Union.) I was determined on my side not to be banished, but to keep on figuring in the lives of the people I loved, first and foremost you and your sister, but also, importantly, my students. Since by any conventional reckoning I did not have the means to live, Lynn and I had to move so often we did not qualify as having an address. My continuing to show up for you, Margie, and my students felt a bit magical, like materializing out of nowhere. Because this all happened contrary to the wishes of certain overseers (your mother wanted me in jail; the chairman wanted me gone), my time with all of you felt a trifle stolen— musically *rubato*. Is this beginning to sound rabbity?

My only friend in the area—a deep secret—happened to be the last of an authentic (grandmother-trained) line of witches from Grafton County. She also had a master's degree in psychology. "Double trouble" is, as you know, the witch's element. My transformation from a straight-ahead lecturer on Plato (I functioned as the ambassador from Plato's *Republic* to the Ivy League in northern New England) into an intractable imitator of Socrates all took place under the tutelage of this woman. I changed from someone with a very predictable schedule to someone who was generally out of place (*atopos*, as they said of the real Socrates). I also developed a free-range tongue. The psychiatrist who officiated my case called it a "conversion." My friend taught me to resist more and obey less. When the bad times really hit, she was my main means of invisible support, regularly coming up with little bundles of cash (a few hundred dollars at a time), which she assured me she won at the racetrack through doses of witchcraft. I believed her—and still do. She won my trust in this matter one afternoon in the anxious days before the trip to Edinburgh where our family was going to fall apart. She took me out to the golf course behind the college to say goodbye and to adjust my attitude toward money—she knew that my mother had inspired in me a lifelong fear of poverty. She had with her a thousand dollars in tens and twenties of which she proposed to give me five hundred, but only after I had ripped up the first five hundred and thrown the pieces into the wind. This was like the sermon on the fairway; I can still see the five hundred bucks blowing away from me. It was she who presented me, some months after I acquired the first Rabbit, with Brown Bunny. I knew by this time that if she gave you an object (a figurine, say), it was to a point. It was to be *used*. I can still feel her ire over my careless handling of a jade elephant she gave me to get through the time abroad. Brown Bunny became at once my bedside icon until Margie winkled him out of my bedroom in Baltimore. Mind you, forces from my childhood were at this time beginning to reestablish themselves in my life. Like a good American I had been trampling them since the time of my marriage. I became a grim, lockstep adult who did not cry and had no eye for tenderness between people. I have subsequently learned to cry every day and melt when I behold human kindness. I grew up on the projected love of my stuffed animals—and I currently live on what I call the "hug line" (Check out the lyrics to "Chega de Saudade.") Of course, during my married years I was a materialist who had no commerce with the preternatural and certainly did not believe in witches. So the coming to the fore of Brown Bunny was a big event. Shortly before he became the protector of my sleep, I had taken another conspicuous step in the direction of animism. I gave my new Rabbit a name—Mad Dog—something I had never done with any of my previous cars and did only one more time with the second Rabbit, which I christened Chief. As you know, both were nicknames of basketball players I loved at the time (Fred Carter and Robert Parish), both of whom had attributes laid up in their nicknames that I wanted for myself: Mad Dog for the first half of visitation and Chief for the second half. (Your mother and stepfather played like Bill Laimbeer.) I suppose the case would have looked neater if I had named the cars Fiver and Hazel, but *Watership Down* has no connection to Brer Rabbit. Something was afoot and the inexorability of it depended upon its unfolding beneath the level where things are made neat. Had there been a car from Greece called the Elenchus (the Refutation), I would have campaigned for that. I know now that my identification with Socrates was not as primary as my identification with Brer Rabbit. In order to protect her privacy, I have been tempted to refer to the last witch from Grafton County as Diotima, because she taught me a lot about love. But given that she did a great job protecting me, she should have the name of the Witch-Rabbit who looked out for Brer Rabbit—Mammy-Bammy Big-Money.

I would never have wanted a bust of Socrates standing just off my pillow. The rabbit-holes of retreat, coziness, and sleep were just the sort of thing Socrates used to block for his interlocutors. Anyway, witches do not number cross-examiners among their familiars.

I hope this little review has made it seem as though the rabbit between us was gestating right from the beginning. Maybe from that ultimate worst moment when our eyes met for the last time as the taxi was pulling away from our apartment in Edinburgh, and you climbed into the rear window for one more goodbye and we shared a look—a streak across your face—that made me know that you knew this was going to be awful. Rabbit tokens passed between us for the next thirty-three years right up to your postcard of Esterhazy leaving his family. Later I'll tell the story of how a large stuffed rabbit that I gave you wound up—against your will—starring as the Velveteen Rabbit in a school stageplay you attended. On the back of the postcard you wrote, "I hate that I have been leaving you for over thirty years. I hate visitation." Perhaps you and I first bonded in the subversive world of animal fables through the bedtime stories I used to tell you about the various scrapes, good times, and close calls that befell a little girl named Sweetie (= you) and a raccoon named Herman (= me), who used to come to her window at night and get her to sneak out and have adventures. In those first cold weeks back in New England, when Lynn and I had no car, we were living in two rooms in a farmhouse up Route 5 in North Thetford. How anything was going to work out was completely unclear. The only answer we had was that we were within walking distance of a grocery store. Having lost important parts of myself—you and Margie—I was going to have to subconsciously refind Brer Rabbit, who had helped me with the suppression of my grandmother. The idea of buying a Volkswagen Rabbit began in North Thetford. One very clear and cold night Lynn and I were walking up Route 5 carrying groceries, and the sky was flooded with stars. I looked up and made out the profile of a rabbit. I then decided latently to crib a motto from the emperor Constantine, who while gazing at the vault of the heavens saw a crucifix: *In hoc signo visitabitis* (In this sign you will visit). So the rabbit emerged as the symbol of our visitation. I began to see glimmers of a future.

Earlier I spoke of my choice of a Rabbit as *demonic*, that, like Osiris, I wanted to get "inside" a rabbit; as a Platonist, I could just as well have said "inside the Form of the Rabbit." Eventually I will make it clear that this is not superstition, not impenetrably mysterious, and not crazy. For the time being we can lean on Wittgenstein. In my favorite short work of his, *Remarks on Frazer's* Golden Bough, he proposes the following free-standing thought: "And magic always rests on the idea of symbolism and of language." The idea of a symbol, which we will investigate later, can lead us out of the woods and into the briar patch. "Rabbit" names a concept in English comprising a large number of language-games which elude our attention, concerning which Wittgenstein says later in the same work, "a whole mythology is deposited in our language."

So our relationship was going to have to be stuffed into the word "visitation." Let's look for a moment at the roots of the explosive little verb "visit." It comes from the Latin *visito*, meaning to go to see. "Visit" is a verb that seems to have taken shape in two stages. It is the frequentative form (which denotes the aspect of an action's being *recurrent* or *repeated*) of the verb *visere,* which means *to look at attentively, behold,* which in turn is the intensive form of the verb *videre,* to see. No wonder your mother complained about my getting so much "quality time"; and in their letter to the court, they objected to the "onslaught of attention" you received when you were with me.

We visited.

They should have done their homework.

The two automobiles, Mad Dog and Chief, were not just nominally rabbits, bearing a little logo fastened on to the back of the car (a logo that, coming as it did from Germany, looked more like a hare than a rabbit). In fact they carried out one of the symbolic rules of the rabbit in very important ways. Showing how this was so should take us right up to the threshold of our question: What are symbols and how do they work? (But before that we will take a gander at *Harvey.*)

One of the oldest legendary attributes of the rabbit (which we have already touched on), attested in cultures all over the world, is the rabbit as INTERCESSOR or GO-BETWEEN. Shi'ite peasants in Anatolia explain that it is forbidden for them to eat rabbit (or hare), because the rabbit is the incarnation of Ali, the intercessor between Allah and the faithful. This ties up with a saying of the Bektāshī dervishes, "Muhammad is the chamber and Ali is the doorway." Ali, the cousin and son-in-law of Muhammad, moved the government of Islam out of Arabia and into southern Iraq, the newly conquered zone at the edge of the former Persia. For the overwhelming majority of Shi'ites, the privilege of the true intercessor is claimed exclusively for Ali's son, Hosain. Hosain returned to the area hoping to lead a revolt and was brutally slaughtered at Karbala when the Partisans of Ali (Shi'ite) failed to rally to the cause. His death is the central religious mystery of Shi'ism, and at the passion play performed every year in his honor on the tenth day of Muharram, he too is referred to as a doorway at the gate of Paradise.

The story of Ali—amplified by the story of Hosain—helps us to see what is nearly universally sensed about the rabbit when it is cast in the role of intercessor. First of all, an intercessor covers the distance or gap between worlds, a world being a presumptively self-sufficient area of life closed off from interlopers and contamination by higher laws. The second thing an intercessor does is to carry the clues, the proximity, to a better way of life. Rabbits have been opening human hearts for centuries and, indeed, look like little wickets leading to a world of love. An intercessor is an elastic part of the border who shows up in your vicinity bearing a look-see at paradise. How is it that rabbits tap into our hearts? I think the answer lies in rabbit phenomenology. But a zoologist named Dan Graur has suggested that our link is through DNA. In a 1996 article in *Nature,* he argued on the basis of DNA analysis that, after tree shrews and flying lemurs, primates are closer to lagomorphs (the rabbit family) than to any other mammalian order. Be advised that one such intercession of great moment for children took place at the end of the nineteenth and the beginning of the twentieth century, in English-speaking cultures where children tended to be seen as chattel. We rode the crest of that intercession straight through the visitation years.

One of the most definitive distortions that your mother enforced on visitation was that under no circumstances would she deliver you to or pick you up from at my house. Her refusal to cooperate included even halfway measures such as dropping you at the Hanover Inn when my car had broken down in town. "Visitation is your responsibility. Get a taxi or forget about it!" This rule meant that the deep form of visitation and everything implied thereby was that of *me-coming-for-you*. And since the distances were always too far to walk, the form was further determined as *me-coming-for-you-in-a-car*. So the Rabbits, Mad Dog and Chief, were what intercession looked like from the outside (something for you to know and me to imagine) and felt like from the inside. Because of threats that could swoop down anytime from the throne of your mother, I was always nervous and jumpy on the trip out to get you. My darkest fear was that visitation would be summarily called off and not rescheduled, but thanks to the two of you, this never happened. When I finally arrived, pulled into the yard, and gave the obligatory toot, the scene that followed—the "transfer"—was positively spooky. There could be no overt display of excitement or affection in front of your mother, since that might provoke an "incident" or have repercussions when you got back home Sunday evening. You and Margie went about the business of hauling your things from the house to the car like somber little automatons, all the while signaling eyerolls, little snorts and grunts, and secret sighs that the whole thing was a charade. Lynn and I were unable to help, because there was an understanding that we were not allowed to get too close to the house. On top of this, we often had to deal with something hollered to you from the back door, some urgent message or a new set of

34

orders that your mother demanded that one of you deliver before anything else happened. We all got to be expert at containing these little hand grenades that your mother would lob out to the car—like visitation should start with her imperious voice. Once we shut the door of the car, the current of love began to flow and we were visiting before we left the property.

The Rabbit had a door to a higher form of life.

A Little Brief against the Book That Ruined Us in Court

"Woe to you! for you are like graves which are not seen, and men walk over them without knowing it."
One of the lawyers answered him, "Teacher, in saying this you reproach us also." And he said, "Woe to you lawyers also! for you load men with burdens hard to bear, and you yourselves do not touch the burdens with one of your fingers. Woe to you! for you build the tombs of the prophets whom your fathers killed."
—Luke 11:44–47

When I was forced by the court to hire an attorney *ad litem* for the two of you, he relied on a trilogy of books—the central volume being *Beyond the Best Interests of the Child*—which enabled him to keep his fingers clear of our burden. He never gave any evidence of having read my one hundred and thirty-page narrative-analysis of all the abuse your mother and stepfather heaped on our contact with one another. Because Anna Freud is one of the coauthors of the trilogy, along with Joseph Goldstein and Albert J. Solnit, they claim their guidelines are "psychoanalytically informed." A more accurate description would be psychoanalytically hobbled. As they say early in the book, "We have a preference for privacy." (This when a Denver group of pediatricians, using x-rays as objective proof, had already brought the new scourge of the Battered Child Syndrome to light.) They believe that custodial parents must suffer no breach in their autonomy. They also believe that "the noncustodial parent should have no legally enforceable right to visit the child." Because they saw harm as inherent in every violation of family integrity, they "decided to err on the side of non-intrusiveness." And they did. This is a straight inheritance from Sigmund Freud, a great keeper of secrets and hypervigilant about non-interference—anything that might diminish the transference. Later in their book the sacrosanct word "autonomy" degenerates into "authority." Authority that craves privacy is likely to be flawed and harboring a secret. Are flaws and secrets good for children? No one ever entered our house who might abridge my parents' authority; that is, they had no friends. I grew up like Allison Mackenzie of *Peyton Place*—she, too, was illegitimate. She finished off her sense of this by finding the empty and friendless house she was raised in "queer" and "all wrong." I felt the peculiarity of the ground rules of my house to be a birthmark-like taint on me. In retrospect, I can see that I was always looking to be adopted into a normal family. (My theme song was: "How much is that doggie in the window, / The one with the waggily tail.") Didn't you feel a little like this too, because your mother and stepfather demanded your support for their game of making your sister feel unwanted? When my filial desire to become an MD withered on the vine, it was replaced by the fantasy vocation of being a full-time brilliant houseguest.

Another implicit defect in the trilogy is that it does nothing to supplement Freud's *libidinal* concept of love. Love in Freud is like a river that flows from a sexual underground leading to feelings, urges, inclinations, and passions, all of which are opaque and occasionally thin out into unrecognizable forms of self-love. This meant that the attorney *ad litem* followed up all the psychosexual accusations that your mother and stepfather saw fit to sling at us. Did we engage in sexualized wrestling with the children? Did I give sexualized baths to Margie? Were we promoting lesbianism by buying you a sportcoat? I can say with an absolutely clean conscience that there were no overtones of sexuality in any of our activities. The two of you never complained about us giving you the creeps, though your sister did about your stepfather. Margie's mother never bathed her. She showed up for each visit with hair that needed to be washed and nails that needed to be trimmed. Thanks to Freud's impoverished ideas about love, the attorney passed over all the evidence I supplied him of there being no *will* on the part of your mother and stepfather to love Margie: no solicitude, no compassion, no forbearance, no gentleness, nothing festive. Your mother's love of you was shot full of holes by her incessant comparison of you to other people. In the words of Søren Kierkegaard, with which I am sure you will agree, "comparison is like the hidden worm which consumes in secret and does not die, before it has taken the life out of love."

A third lapse descended from Freud is the three authors' professed inability to know children: "To arrive at a trustworthy opinion of a particular child's true mental state as to who are his psychological parents is a matter which taxes the skills of even the most experienced clinicians." In 1897, writing to his friend Wilhelm Fliess, Freud abandoned the hypothesis of "infantile seduction," meaning that adults were the initiators of sexual abuse. He replaced it with a hybrid concept—*psychical reality*—in which truth and fantasy coincide. Freud was able to live with this vacillation because he had a solipsistic theory of speech where the therapeutic value of speaking consisted in getting the words *out*. He did not realize that a sentence had to be brought to completion in the understanding of a listener. Your attorney fell into this conceptual impasse. He never took seriously your plainspoken desire for more visitation and to have the weird restrictions removed from me. (I was forbidden to approach either of you at school functions and from meeting the parents of your friends. They made up all kinds of rules that would keep me, in their words, a "social outcast.") Margie—who by then felt herself to be an entirely secondary person in her home—was on record as having requested a change of custody, for which she paid dearly. That request was never given any scope in the courtroom. For your participation on my side of the lawsuit, your mother called you "Nazi children!" That was one of her hundreds of documented cruelties that, because of her "autonomy," she never had to answer for.

The last echo from Freud in the books is of his cultural pessimism. The authors ridicule words like "ideal" and "best," contending that to use such words will contaminate with "hope" and "magic." They even go so far as to say: "there is no societal consensus about what is 'best' or even 'good' for all children." They do not bother to ask who is spending millions of dollars to wreck the consensus. Can your mother's depraved remark in defense of Margie's latchkey status be heard without a critical reflex? "It's good for a child to stay in the house alone and do nothing." As an eight-year-old, Margie was generally frightened. Is that good? The authors are looking for the "least detrimental alternative," which they see presumptively as belonging to the *status quo,* "however unsatisfactory that might be." Theirs is an ethic of minimizing evil. Like all other moral theories that concentrate on reducing the negative—starting with Thomas Hobbes and his mythical war of all against all—they make space for the conceptual substitution of things (commodities/property) for people. According to Erik Erickson, "the devoutly skeptical Freud proclaimed that man's uppermost duty was *das leben auszuhalten*: to stand up to life, to hold out." Not "to live," a verb that has almost no content in Freud. But one might say with Kierkegaard that a human's highest duty is to love one's neighbors, to identify with them, and to respect their dignity. "Love is not an exclusive characteristic, but it is a characteristic by which or in virtue of which you exist for others."

In attempting to wrap a legal membrane around the family, the authors remain sublimely silent about how corporations are pounding away at children. Through television, schools, and hired "alpha" youths who serve as itinerant endorsers, "a major thrust of contemporary marketing to children is the interposition of the marketer between the parent and the child. Marketers create utopian spaces free of parents and employ insidious dual messaging strategies. Ads position the marketer with the child against the parent." Seventy-five percent of U.S. children between the ages of six and twelve say, above all, they want to be rich, and sixty-one percent to be famous. As Juliet B. Schor says, "The bottom line on the culture they're being raised in is that it's a lot more pernicious than most adults have been willing to admit." Studies have concluded that "people with higher financial aspirations scored lower on measures of self-actualization and vitality. They also had lower levels of community affiliation. . . . Materialism is related to psychological distress and difficulty adapting to life."

Finally, there are some egregious falsehoods floating through the books. The authors claim that "children have no psychological conception of relationship by blood-tie until quite late in their development." I know that from early on I was sensitive to physical comparisons with my adoptive parents. Margie discovered happily at a young age that she and I both had hitchhiker's thumb and brown eyes. A few pages later, the authors write that an immature child tends to ignore the admission of adoption. That is because such a child is very busy mentally securing a biological tie. They assert the ability to identify who among personally available adults is or has the capacity to become a psychological parent and thus will enable a child to feel wanted. Their complacent formula for this judgment is to stick with the custodial parent. They also allege that "meaningful visits for the child can only occur if both the custodial and noncustodial parents are of a mind to make them work." We always had a great time visiting, even though the two of you were catechized immediately before and after.

III

I NEVER SAW *HARVEY*

Harvey debuted on Broadway in 1944, the year I was born. Six years later it was playing at a downtown movie theater in Buffalo, New York. It was not the kind of film that my father would take us to. I now own the DVD and watch it as a story that always improves my spirits. I once loaned it to a psychother-apist and—believe it or not—he had a hard time giving it back. I used to enjoy stopping by his office and asking if he had Harvey with him. With the stageplay and movie, a much larger version of the rabbit that concerns us made an historic break into adult America. Love and kindness on the loose. It should have started a cult; but, alas, it proved to be a one-time affair (a kind of *hapax legomenon,* as they say of an expression that Homer only uses once—I indulge this bit of pedantry because it sounds like a species of rabbit). The spirit of Harvey was beaten down by psychotropic drugs. Harvey possessed a new attribute that was an inspired extension of the rabbits children had learned to love. Harvey could fill your speech up with warmth and pleasantness. At the end of Act II in the play Elwood, Harvey's disciple, says to Kelly, the psychiatric nurse, "Quite sure—but ask me again, anyway, won't you? I liked that warm tone you had in your voice just then." To which Dr. Sanderson, her potential boyfriend, adds (*without realizing he is saying it*), "So did I." At the end of this chapter we will explore how the VW Rabbits lived up to this attribute.

Harvey is about a 6 foot 3½ inch (not including ears) invisible rabbit and the constant companion of forty-two-year-old Elwood P. Dowd (Jimmy Stewart), since sometime after his mother's death. She died in his arms when he was in his thirties (*Pietà* in reverse). Harvey is a "pooka," defined in the movie as coming from "Old Celtic mythology, a fairy spirit in animal form, always very large. The pooka appear here and there, now and then, to this one and that one. A benign, but mischievous creature, very fond of rumpots and crackpots." We would do well to understand those last two terms as a modern translation of "publicans and sinners." *Harvey* is a genuine fable-form of the gospel story, starring a supernatural rabbit akin to Puck in Shakespeare's *A Midsummer Night's Dream*. As in the New Testament, Elwood represents the will of a divinity whom he communicates with; and the more you believe in Elwood and Harvey, the better you get. The plot turns on Elwood and Harvey's practice, mostly based in a downtown bar called Charlie's, where they play the jukebox and are radically pleasant to whomever they happen to meet. As Elwood states late in the movie, in response to being encouraged to feel righteous indignation toward his sister, Veta, who has almost succeeded in having him committed to the local asylum, Chumley's Rest, "My mother used to say to me, 'In this world you must be oh so smart or oh so pleasant.' Well, for years I was smart. I recommend pleasant."

Harvey does not make any appearances in the movie (with the exception of the oil portrait of him with Elwood), but he did at the end of the Broadway production. Unless he is declared to be absent or missing, Harvey typically inhabits the space choreographed by Elwood's gestures. Harvey generally cannot be heard either. People gather what he is saying in the same way that they infer the other end of an overheard cellphone conversation, but with one gargantuan difference—they are included in the conversation. Conversation is the principal medium of their radical pleasantness, along with Elwood's hospitality since he invites everyone he meets to dinner at his house. "Harvey and I," says Elwood, "warm ourselves in golden moments of talk"; when those whom they have befriended "tell about the big terrible things they have done. The big wonderful things they *will* do. Their hopes, their regrets, their loves, their hates. All very large because nobody ever brings anything small into a bar."

He may hang out in bars, but Elwood is no rumpot (drunkard); and while he is definitely on a collision course with the nearby sanitarium—"I've wrestled with reality for thirty-five years and I'm happy to state I've finally won out over it"—he's no crackpot. He is prepared to go the distance with kindness. Before R. D. Laing and the Anti-Psychiatry movement, there was *Harvey*. Over the course of the movie, we watch as Elwood and the big white rabbit with their tactics of openness and benevolence consistently outflank and eventually prevail over a psychiatry that tells lies, violates one's confidence, is sex-obsessed, and resolutely impersonal. In the final analysis, it's ready to inject you with a faith-destroying serum—formula 977—after which "you won't see the rabbit anymore, but you will see your responsibilities and duties." By the end of the movie the head of the sanitarium where Elwood was to be committed has himself seen the pooka and turns to Elwood, who had already told him about Harvey earlier in the day, for more guidance. Dr. Chumley now learns about two of Harvey's occult powers, both of which seem to me to touch right on the pulse of the projection of the rabbit into the adult world. Harvey can see into the future, unexpected things that are going to happen to people. He can also stop clocks. As Elwood explains, science has overcome time and space, "but Harvey has overcome not only time and space, but any objections." Inasmuch as Harvey works his magic as a wholly entailed interlocutor, we should imagine his special effects as arising out of conversation to which he is a party. I am inclined to see these two occult powers as directly antagonistic to Freud. He insisted throughout his career on the *scientific* status of psychoanalysis but repeatedly washed his hands of any capacity for predicting. Freud also elaborated a concept of psychotherapy that was sacramentally bound to the clock. The gift of prophecy does not come through the immediacy of the eye but through the augury of the ear. Harvey listens into the future with his outsized rabbit-attachment to humanity.

Psychoanalysts pride themselves on their ability to listen. They refer to their form of attention as free-floating or evenly suspended. Ultimately it is an edited and unnatural way to listen. They highlight "slurs, stumblings, mumbling, garbled speech, spoonerisms, pauses, slips, ambiguous phrasing, double and triple entendres"—everything that goes wrong. They are trained to shut down the ear that listens for meaning so as not to "understand" a story told by a neurotic. They look for the nervous content of what you have said and are armed with a theory that enables them to reconstruct what is on your unconscious mind. A psychoanalyst is not present to the deliberative or active part of your soul, so you might as well be a slave. That's why predictions elude them. Mary Chase, who wrote *Harvey,* was careful to connect her rabbit to slavery. She twice has Veta refer to the orderly at Chumley's Rest as a white slaver. Of course, racist Hollywood cut this.

Elwood and Harvey are not ordinary self-centered listeners. They have already identified with their interlocutors, so they hear through love (which is the highest form of knowledge). This is why people are able to expand and say something "large" about themselves. They do not feel compartmentalized (your stepfather's favorite terrain) and hedged in by other people's interests. Anyone who is out on the town is always like an epic *in medias res* and it takes a loving muse for them to tell where they are. Harvey through Elwood says "I'll do anything for you." A psychoanalyst cannot.

Everyone knows that hardly anything has a more corrosive effect on a conversation than one of the parties to it attending to the clock, i.e., the necessity to keep things short or the feeling that there's no time to get into this or that. Everyone also knows that after the best conversations, one returns to the clock wondering where all the time went but also bolstered against "any objections." One has just spent time *living*. Rabbits have a special relation to time. They make the present tense more commodious. Earlier I referred to the rabbit as the lord of deixis: the rabbit declares *now* and *here* with its whole being. As a matter of fact, anyone in the presence of a big animal breathing can feel oneself being lifted off the tenterhooks of clocktime. Harvey does not only appear to Elwood; his sister Veta reports occasional sightings, and Dr. Chumley has an extended session with him. We can suppose that he sometimes materializes and speaks to the people with whom Elwood engages in conversation. Seeing a beautiful bunny who is bigger than you and actually says "I will do anything for you" would likely throw you back to childhood when you entered your bedroom and saw the warm expressions on your stuffed animals and they became your confidantes. Harvey and Elwood are enchanting enough to roll back the stone in front of the entrance to what St. Augustine calls the cave of the self. Parts of yourself that have lived in abeyance now get to consciously enter a kindly present.

This is what the whole *Harvey* incursion was about—new territory for rabbithood, new territory for the invitations of rabbithood. And, by the way, there are strong hints in the movie that this territory (in keeping with the spirit of the rabbit) is non-patriarchal. In a wonderful *tour de force,* Veta referring over her shoulder to a painting of her mother ("the pride of the family") explains the difference between a "fine oil painting" and a "mechanical thing like a photograph." Unbeknownst to her, Elwood has, since she was last in the room, placed a portrait of himself and Harvey in front of the painting of their mother. As Veta puts it, "the photograph shows only the reality. The painting shows not only the reality, but the dream behind it." So the dream "behind" Harvey is maternal, which is very much in keeping with the rabbit's ancient, fabled association with the Earth Mother and the Moon, and latterly with the likes of Hecate clear down to Beatrix Potter. (Peter Rabbit's father was put in a pie by Mrs. McGregor. Brer Rabbit has lots of "little rabs" but there is nothing peremptory about him. It wasn't until Richard Adams' *Watership Down* that we encountered rabbits with a masculine feel.) Another very pointed overture occurs toward the end of *Harvey* when Dr. Chumley has himself taken to the couch and is telling his secret dreams to Elwood who, of course, listens attentively but then ever so gently advises him that he is "making a mistake not allowing the woman [in his fantasy] to talk."

Harvey obviously failed to colonize America. The idea of mobile rabbit locutories—rabbit parlors—never caught on, and Harvey was largely (could we say "smally"?) forgotten. (I should tell you I once proposed to a committee in Washington investigating the "usefulness" of the humanities that people trained in the humanities should be stationed in "talk booths" throughout the country so as to assist people who were feeling their imagination for humanity running near empty.) But it was not only *Harvey* who lost. All forms of talk therapy were attacked under the rubric that they "take too much time"; and going for therapy came sadly to mean seeing someone who owned the big Book of Runes (the *DSM*), who had prescription-writing powers, and sent you off to the drugstore.

Before moving on, I would like to respond parable-style to someone who objects that rabbits have not disappeared from the adult world, but rather have made beachheads via cartoons and the Energizer Bunny. In *Harvey* Elwood does the animating—not Chuck Jones or a couple of D batteries, nor women walking around serving in bunny-outfits on orders from Hef.

"Mobile rabbit locutories" or "rabbit parlors" puts me in mind of the high-spirited conversations we used to have in the VW Rabbits. They were never confrontational or sour. This was no accident. The aptness of cars for good, mutually revelatory conversation has long been understood by my favorite living movie director, the Iranian Abbas Kiarostami. He has made one movie, *Ten*, set entirely inside a car, and another, *The Taste of Cherry*, predominantly within a car. In a commentary on *Ten* he described the aesthetic virtues built in, as it were, to the cell of a car, some of them special to movie-making but most of them applicable to us. Cars are intimate. The people sit next to instead of opposite one another and this, according to Kiarostami, creates the "right mood for dialogue." Stretches of being by oneself, bits of reverie, can easily alternate and mix in with the talk. Looking out the window has the tendency to bring subjectivity to the foreground, and once there, a lot of conversation can be suspended from it. A point I am not sure Kiarostami made, but am certain he appreciates, is that people driving together in a car are doing something together. They are looking at roughly the same things as they do it. This brings their manifolds of sensation into an unusual congruence—like the experience in a movie theater, minus the fact that what they see is not being directed at them for their entertainment and there is no rule of silence. This clearly does not mean that things always go well in the car, but that they do come out. That was how we discovered so much about one another.

Coda Bianca

Some years ago back on High Pastures Road, I used to spend a good amount of time looking through the windows at the hay fields outside our house, daydreaming about a particular movie of Kiarostami's, *The Wind Will Carry Us*. As you know, I named a beautiful silver maple tree that reached out onto Route 107, the Kiarostami Tree. Last year they cut it back, but this spring the tree has decided to reach out again. Eventually I wrote a little verse to him that never left my notebook. I wonder in the spirit of Elwood—who said: ". . . the evening wore on. A nice expression. With your permission, I'm going to say it again. The evening wore on,"—if I might write it here and share it with you.

To Abbas
When the hay is old enough to wave
And accept a brushing from the wind,
It waves away America
And Iran comes rushing in.

IV

WHAT IS A SYMBOL

The word symbol is a term of such Protean elusiveness
that my instinct, as a practical literary critic, has always
been to avoid it as much as possible.

—Northrop Frye, "The Symbol as a Medium of Exchange"

Since a certain symbol has ensconced itself in the middle of our
life, it seems to me that we will have to go after this elusive term.
Even though it is a notorious snark—and the original *Hunting
of the Snark* ended in the baffling result that the Snark was a
Boojum—I propose that we pursue the meaning of "symbol" the
way they pursued the Snark, "with forks and hope."

I am no philologist, but looking at the history of the word
"symbol," it is almost as if its meaning did not want to be found
out. Usually when one consults the etymology of a word, one
will be led to, as J. L. Austin puts it, an old idea which has pervaded and governed all the changes, extensions, and additions to
the word over its history. But the most distinctive and profound
idea associated with our word "symbol"—the one which enables
us to say unequivocally of either a national flag, a disco-ball, a

handshake, a swastika, a kiss, a crucifix, or a rabbit, that each is a symbol—that idea is not clearly visible in the ancient and classical Greek from which our word derives. In fact, the idea we are after does not seem to take up residence under the root term for "symbol" until quite late, when *symbolon* is used to denote the distinctive mark of Christians. This does not mean that the Greeks were in any way unfamiliar with symbols or symbolic behavior. Their culture and landscape abounds with both: pouring libations, the authority of the scepter, tripods, the statues of Winged Victory (*Nikē*) all over the Acropolis, animal sacrifice, herms used as boundary markers, the great robe of Athena and the procession that carried it. The symbolic is everywhere but not denominated as such. I have a guess as to why this was so. Being inducted into the use of a symbol is not like learning a word (*pace* Wittgenstein). Symbols lack the neutrality of words. Different symbols have different apprenticeships. Maybe even more telling is that while the meaning of a word stays relatively constant, the sense and force of a symbol can fluctuate greatly with the passage of time. Thus the conditions for bringing the symbolic realm under a single definitional eye were less than ideal.

A more severe problem, however, was waiting down the road: a kind of trap. Once it became possible to call symbols and symbolic behavior by a single name, a certain spurious feature of symbols came to the fore, and has obstructed our view of the deep operation of symbols ever since. For any given symbol it is a pretty routine matter to say what it is "a symbol of" or what it "symbolizes." The cross symbolizes Christianity, a kiss is a symbol of affection, the rabbit a symbol of visitation. Symbols are assimilated to language, to "meaning." Like letters of the alphabet, they degenerate into signs. Does someone waving the Stars and Stripes *mean* "America"?

An anecdote from the best book I ever read on symbolism—*Rethinking Symbolism* by Dan Sperber—will make this problem clear. Among the Ndembu of Zambia is a certain tree, the *museng'u,* which evidently because of its etymology and also because of the quantity of fruit it bears, has come to symbolize a "multiplicity of kills" when hunting. As Sperber says, "When the Ndembu wish to mean 'a multiplicity of kills,' they simply use the words of their language, and not a branch of *museng'u.* They use the latter when they wish not to mean, but to obtain 'game in abundance.'" Years before reading this I had found and copied out a similar thought about the portentous nature of symbols, spoken by a character in Robert Musil's *Man Without Qualities*: "every symbol must in due course turn into something real; that is to say, I can let myself be deeply moved by a symbol without necessarily understanding it, but after a while I am bound to turn away from the mirror of my heart and get something else done, something I have meanwhile found needs doing." In fact, despite all of the false leads and blind alleys (one of the worst being the Freudian approach), one writer after another has found that more than just signifying something (e.g. ☮ = "peace") *symbols work on you.*

I remember the amazing sense of relief Lynn and I felt when we crossed into a nearly flag-free Canada in the spring of 2002 when the War on Terror had stuck flags up and down every street in America. I understood then why the banners carried by the Roman legions were called *vexilla.* I also understood that even though an irritating symbol may make you murmur in its presence because of what it "signifies," the fact that you keep on murmuring and feeling irritated proves that something more than saying or signifying is going on. A symbol cannot be managed like a sentence in the language. It cannot be reasoned with, refuted, qualified, etc., the way a piece of speech can. This implies that a symbol is less than rational. I found that the only effective way to argue with a symbol is to interfere with its transmission—rip it down, burn it, or upstage it with some larger countersymbol. [A brief aside: symbols do not really have contraries unless by prior arrangement (e.g.,✝, ☪, ✿)]. For me the rabbit as a symbol is just about the polar opposite of the Stars and Stripes. While I always envied your mother's position as the custodial parent (and took her to court to try to divest her of it), I confess that there was one custodial obligation I was secretly glad not to have to participate in. As the visiting parent, I never had to surrender you on a daily basis to that big psychological slaughterhouse with the flagpole in front of it: SCHOOL. Seeing you over school distances—crowds in front of the main door, buses, school plays, rugby games, graduation ceremonies—always put me on the verge of tears. Let that stand for my *ir*-responsibility.

I HOPE that you are now comfortable with the idea that symbols operate on you, and that some of the other strange things that have been said over the centuries about symbols will, if not make sense, at least feel right. Goethe thought of a true symbol as a "living momentary revelation of the Inscrutable." That sounds a lot like what I was trying to say at the beginning about the bunny on the train. Goethe also referred to a symbol encountered at a specific time and place as a "pregnant moment."

A symbol is not there to give birth to interpretations. Not only does no amount of interpretation exhaust a living symbol, but like "The Star Spangled Banner" or the Sign of the Cross ("*In nomine patris,*" etc.), they just get added to the symbols themselves. Symbols are agglomerative, and as Coleridge phrased it, symbols "remain inexpressible," that is, nothing will let the expressiveness out of a symbol. Symbols are there to give birth to something else: good hunting, good visitation, good citizens. According to medieval historian Johan Huizinga, "symbolism is a very profound function of the mind"; their effect on us is tacit and not open to conscious fiddle-faddle. If having seen a certain symbol, I now feel like behaving in a particular manner, I may set about that behavior with no thought or recollection of having just seen the symbol. Even if I am vaguely aware of a symbol's having prompted me to do something, I may not in the least be able to explain why or provide some middle term linking the symbol and the action. "I don't know, it just made me feel like calling you." This means that we will have to revise Samuel Beckett's maxim, "No symbol where none intended." Symbols sneak up on you.

Although we are normally in the dark about how symbols work on us, and sometimes do not even so much as recognize that an item before us is indeed a symbol, nonetheless, symbols do need to be noticed, if not remarked. Thus the most effective symbols have long been appreciated for their capacity to stand out and focus the attention, to lift themselves because of their form and placement out of the flux of perception. Jungians describe this as the "numinosity" of a symbol. Nature may abhor a vacuum, but it is the mission of every symbol to create one— to create its own little dance floor and call you onto it. Going back to the Ndembu for a moment, when they want to refer to what we think of as a symbol, they use the word *chijikijilu,* or "a landmark." This seems like a much better clue to what a symbol is than our word which pulls us toward the dead horse of "meaning"—which, if you do not mind, I will take one more whack at. As a rule, when we want to establish what a given word, phrase, or sentence means, we have to consider the context in which it occurred. By contrast, symbols (e.g. crystal balls, scales of justice, mistletoe) with their isolate hyperclarity tell us what the context is.

I think it is time for us to pick up our FORKS. Does that mean we are going to define "symbol"? No, but we are going to get close enough to touch it. I owe this insight almost completely to Dan Sperber. The daemonic power of the symbol is closely related to etiquette. Yes, table manners, Emily Post, politeness. In fact all of the latter are indeed thoroughly symbolic, which is why they are easily misunderstood, gainsaid, and abused. The main form that misunderstanding takes is to think of etiquette as nothing but an arbitrary set of rules (salad fork to the left of the dinner fork) and to imagine politeness as nothing more than obeying those rules. But notice that behavior that feels like nothing more than strict compliance with the rules is not felt to live up to the rules. Think of all the ways in which someone can behave correctly but objectionably: no rule is broken but the behavior is perfunctory, mechanical, histrionic, jerky, or sullen. A book of table manners, besides containing rules such as "do not wipe your knife on the tablecloth" or "chew with your mouth closed," also contains the great unwritten injunction: *treat people like this.* In other words, the hope is that one will catch the "spirit" of the rules, internalize them, carry them out not as if they were an imposition but as if they came naturally and were something to build on and embellish. By connecting symbols and etiquette, we are not doing much beyond exploring the links between decor and decorum. To put this all figuratively (which in this instance is not far from literal), a book of etiquette and a symbol both describe circles that elicit an aspiration toward the center. With a written etiquette the center itself is empty, but the momentum towards it is acquired by learning bits of behavior on the periphery—dance steps, manners. The circle of the symbol proper is defined from the center by the evocative reach of the symbol itself—no high-rises in Washington, DC.

How, you may ask, can a symbol induce a style of behavior? Well, pretty much the same way that a book of etiquette can. For either to work they must possess the discernible backing of a *will* that they work. When Jungians refer to the "numinosity" of a symbol, they mean to be describing the sense of it as a manifestation of divine will. A book of etiquette can be said to represent the will of polite society. The charisma of a symbol is very much a matter of the will behind it; and it probably helps if that will is a little obscure, a little dispersed—not traceable to any single, readily identifiable individual. (Gods and royalty are fine.) The will that raised the rabbit over our heads was not mine, not yours, not Margie's, but *ours*. Of course there is still the problem that unlike a book of etiquette, a symbol does not get you started by telling you what to do—although many symbols, like flags and courtrooms, come with their own etiquette, and any strong symbolic arena will have its enforcers, bailiffs, and lictors. What I believe is that a symbol can evoke a style of behavior because lurking around every symbol are unmistakable inducements to *mimēsis*, to imitation. Does that mean we were supposed to imitate rabbits? Well, in fact, we did. Not everything—we did not, despite your mother's efforts, chew pellets. We took on only those aspects that were exemplary for us; we treated the rabbit as a model for emulation (enter Ayatollah Howzyurbuni). When Beatrix Potter was thirty-nine, in a move that inaugurated the slow, grinding break with her parents, she purchased out of her earnings from children's books a farm in the Lake District of England. According to her first biographer, Margaret Lane, "the buying of Hill Top Farm was more, however, far more . . . than a speculation. It was a *symbol* (emphasis added), representing more than one smothered element in her nature. It stood for important decisions and delicate choice, and though decisions and choice produced their fruit only after many years, her emotions about Hill Top were to the end so complex and intense that the sensation of that first break-away . . . never completely faded." Having the duties of a farmer helped her to dissolve the filial piety that kept her imprisoned in her father's home in London, Bolton Gardens, a house with bars on the nursery windows and that made no concessions to children.

Before leaving the subject of symbols, I should declare a source of personal bias that may have worked itself into what I have had to say and very likely had consequences for our life together. One night at the Holiday Inn in White River Junction, Mammy-Bammy Big-Money gave me a Rorschach test, and to gather from the look on her face after it was over, I did not do so well. (Everyone knows you can flunk psychological tests.) When I asked her what was wrong, the only thing she said by way of explanation was that I was "highly given to symbols." Neither of us knew at the time that I had been adopted, an awareness that I like to think might have sweetened the test results. A year ago I came into possession of my "baby book" —a small part of the hoax about my birth status. In it I found my adoptive mother's original "message" to me written in her own hand. It concludes with the sentence, "*There are so many things we have in store for you* [including one falsehood about the size of Moby Dick]—*but first grow up and be a fine gentleman.*" That may not sound like much of a vocation—nowhere near as demanding as what Celia Guevara looked for from her son (I mean to be expressing Che-envy). She meant it, however, and I lived up to it. Throughout my childhood I always found her most present on the other side of a symbol—the tesserae idea—the Christmas tree, Easter baskets, my favorite dinner on my alleged birthday. But I never felt her so close and so pleased as when she would drive me with my white gloves and little blue suit to Driscoll's dancing school on Saturday night. She sometimes came in to watch. This feeling continued on into my adolescent years when she would see me off in my After Six tuxedo to the more grown-up dances at the Nine O'Clock Club. I definitely had my problems with symbols. They could be summed up that the moral of this jingle was lost on me, even though I ate the doughnut:

> Whatever you may do in life,
> Wherever you may go,
> Keep your eye upon the doughnut
> And not upon the hole.

V

DOWN THE PHILOSOPHICAL RABBIT-HOLE
OR "GAVAGAI!"

Rabbits over the centuries have inspired almost no philosophical reflection. This despite the fact that the rabbit life-form has been sensed for quite a while—perhaps as far back as Titian—as an engaging refutation of how we live. I want to be as clear as possible about the fanciful nature of what I have to say. First, there has been a long uncommenced argument between Western Man and the rabbit, which in its unarticulated condition takes the form of what you might call managed (i.e. chronic) discursive tension. Our private thoughts of rabbits unleash in us their "atmosphere" and dead-end uses of the word "cute" and the interjection "aw." Second, since rabbits do not speak, the unjoined argument must be between a modern man and something in him that mumbles appreciatively on behalf of rabbits. Third, the responsibility for maintaining a deaf ear to the rabbit's call to thought has fallen primarily to the discipline of philosophy. The anxiety of denial continues to build up there. (I imagine a revenant Descartes assuring us that what we think are the agonizing screams of a rabbit caught in a steel trap is simply the sound of the trap cutting into its leg bones—the sort of thing he

59

said when he was alive.) Fourth, this whole underground conflict came ever so briefly into the open when a literal rabbit (the detective in me wants to say that they are ideationally the very same rabbit) ran across the two most influential philosophy texts of the mid-twentieth century: Wittgenstein's *Philosophical Investigations* and W. V. O. Quine's *Word and Object*. I think something happened here; but in order to understand this coruscating event, we will have to lean like Socrates did to the Aesop in us. I hope when we are done to have discovered some of the grammar of "rabbit." That will mean that the rabbit has been established in our midst. Here are the passages:

I. I look at an animal; someone asks me: "What do you see?" I answer: "A rabbit."—I see a landscape; suddenly a rabbit runs past. I exclaim: "A rabbit!"

Both things, both the report and the exclamation, are expressions of perception and of visual experience. But the exclamation is so in a different sense from the report: it is forced from us.—It stands to the experience somewhat as a cry to pain.

But since the exclamation is the description of a perception, one can also call it the expression of thought—Someone who looks at an object need not think of it; but whoever has the visual experience expressed by the exclamation is also *thinking* of what he sees.

II. [Quine imagines the situation of a linguist in the jungle attempting to translate the language of a hitherto undiscovered people, what he calls "radical translation."] The utterances first and most surely translated in such a case are ones keyed to present events that are conspicuous to the linguist and his informant. A rabbit scurries by, the native says "Gavagai," and the linguist notes down the sentence "Rabbit" (or, "Lo, a rabbit") as tentative translation, subject to testing in further cases.

For Wittgenstein to liken the exclamation "Rabbit!" to a cry of pain, we must have a profound relation to rabbits, something interior that cannot be kept inside. The language, not voluntary, is pulled out from our depths. He means to contrast this with less engaged situations where the rabbit is not on the loose and recognition of the animal is in question. In Wittgenstein, disengagement from the circumstances of speaking cannot form the basis of our understanding of language, or we will be led to the crazy view that language is fundamentally a matter of looking and naming. Quine was a cornered man. He appealed to the very same running rabbit and its ability to command our attention to pull his theory out of the graveyard. He suppressed the exclamation point because, as a behaviorist, he allows himself to appeal only to the "objective data" available to the linguist translating from scratch, "the forces he sees impinging on the native's surfaces and the observable behavior vocal [phonemic] and otherwise." Under this regimen "Gavagai" is subject to all kinds of ambiguity. It could mean "animal," "white," or "rabbit"; or "rabbit stage," "rabbithood," or "undetached rabbit part"; or "Gavagai" may be the name of the native's pet rabbit, or the name of a neighboring tribe that takes a strange kind of animal with it when it goes on a raid. Quine-style behaviorism excludes observing human expressivity. The linguist violated this rule by writing "lo" in his notebook. Maybe he has a background in anthropology and is more comfortable with humanity afield.

Perhaps he knows that the bulk of the Brer Rabbit stories—which he loves—originated in this region of Africa. He is likely to know that humans do not blurt out "animal" or "white," and he could trust his ear to discern in the native's intonation contour no feeling that his pet had broken free and he was calling it, nor a portent of war. Quine imposes an absurd set of conditions, almost demented, that no one could ever fulfill. Nonetheless, he runs the rabbit by us (stimulus) and out comes "Gavagai" (response), and, lo, we seem to be on our way. But it is all a trick. Even the assumption that the animal is "conspicuous" to both of us—later Quine talks about its being "salient"—seems to overreach the objectively empirical (which usually means judgeable by the eye alone). No wonder Quine refers to it as "so benign a case." It parlays our already developed imagination into the illusion that behaviorism has legs.

For a long time I was reluctant to make anything out of these two cameo appearances, and even more hesitant about entertaining the possibility that they bore intrinsic connections. This ended the day I happened to be looking for something in Paul Bloom's *How Children Learn the Meanings of Words,* and I noticed, evidently for the first time, that the Renaissance painting on the cover of the book had a white rabbit in it. Thanks to Lynn, we were able to identify the painting as Titian's *Virgin and Child with Saint Catherine of Alexandria and a Rabbit* or, simply, *Madonna of the Rabbit.* The book had nothing to say about the choice of a cover, but I could not resist the thought that someone (an editor or Paul Bloom himself) had made another entry on the subject of rabbits and language. In the end, after traveling to Boston to see the painting which happened to

be on exhibit there and was very popular, I decided that the real entry was made by Titian himself. Perhaps Titian, an extremely talented artist with "a very pleasant and vivacious manner" according to Michelangelo, took seriously the opening of the Gospel of John. The Christ child was the bringer of the word and, as such, in him was "life, and the life was the light of men." Could Titian have sensed what Romano Guardini describes as the continual solitude that envelops Jesus, a solitude that "arises because no one understands him. His enemies do not understand, the multitude does not, but neither do his disciples"? At the crux of the painting we are free to imagine that the baby Jesus sees a little bit of himself held before him on the ground by his mother and is breaking free of St. Catherine's arms and his swaddling in order to get down and play with the rabbit. He is clearly not content just to look. I should say that the white of the rabbit is almost otherworldly and singled itself out like no other detail in the entire exhibit (which also included paintings by Veronese and Tintoretto). It will not do to recite the standard iconographic line: "The rabbit represents fecundity." The painting is yet another strong testament to what is beginning to seem like the rabbit's a priori claim on our attention, its pull toward life.

I started to find too much evidence, even if scattered, of a special relation to turn my back on it. Around the same time as the Titian exhibit, I read a remarkable chapter in Italo Calvino's *Marcovaldo* called "The Poisonous Rabbit." Just before Marcovaldo is about to be discharged into the dismal city after a gloomy time in the hospital, he finds a caged rabbit. "There, after days and days of sordid stay in the hospital, at the moment of leaving, he discovered a friendly presence, which would have sufficed to fill his hours and his thoughts. And he had to leave it, go back into the foggy city, where you don't encounter rabbits." All in all, I prefer to follow Wittgenstein's rabbit and to consider how it wrings an exclamation out of us.

In a most interesting book by Michael Thompson, *Life and Action*, he quotes the following passage from Hegel's *Science of Logic* in which Hegel reflects on the hazards of submitting the concept of life to the kind of logical treatment he has in mind:

> The idea of life is concerned with subject matter so concrete, and if you will so real, that with it we may seem to have overstepped the domain of logic as it is commonly conceived. Certainly if logic were to contain nothing but

empty, dead forms of thought, there could be no mention
in it at all of such a content as the idea of life.

Thompson himself agrees with Hegel that thought does,
indeed, take "a quite special turn when it is thought of the living";
and his long essay on this very subject (which I shall refer to
again) proved to be an immense help in thinking about Wittgenstein's "Rabbit!" Thompson does not seem to have appreciated
(he is hardly alone in this) that Wittgenstein accepted the very
same challenge as he and their positions are densely concordant,
even though the *Investigations* is a much more labyrinthine work.
The latter is a warren of thought and completely defies summary.
If one were to choose its most fundamental concept, it would be
the concept of "forms of life." "What has to be accepted, the
given, is—so one could say—*forms of life*." As you probably
know, before he composed the *Investigations,* Wittgenstein wrote
what many—himself included—considered to be the absolute
epitome of the logical view of language and the world, *Tractatus
Logico-Philosophicus*. Toward the end of the book he seems to
have gotten comfortable with Hegel's dilemma. "We feel that
even if *all possible* scientific questions be answered, the problems
of life have still not been touched at all. Of course there is then
no question left, and just this is the answer." A decade or so after
that, he began the immensely subtle and painstaking labor of
recovering for Western thought the long-missing category of
"life." The result, *Philosophical Investigations,* can be thought
of as a long, guided exploration of one juncture after another
in language where we are tempted to form and act on dead,
mechanical pictures of how things work. Wittgenstein's later
work is very *oral*; he believes that talking is the distinctive form

of human life, and that there are so many inhuman ways to talk. We are most alive in a fully acknowledged relationship with a particular person, and the key to this is to be purely responsive to the words and thought of the other without any taint of self-interest. We should think of this as linguistic love. His book is free of ordinary philosophical *rigor mortis*. It is a book about opening yourself up and coming to life.

The running rabbit at the end of the book was no accident. In both volumes of his preliminary studies for Part II of the *Investigations* (*Last Writings*, Volumes I and II), he discusses the "rabbit" exclamation. In Volume I he looks at a rabbit in a cage; his identification is not expressive. Imagine postulating a cage around what someone says to you in a conversation, a cage that will allow your entire understanding to be intellectual and inexpressive. In Volume II he discusses the case of someone who sees a hare run by and doesn't recognize it as a hare. "He proceeds to describe the appearance. Someone else says 'A hare!' and he cannot describe it so precisely." I think Wittgenstein saw in a rabbit dashing across a landscape something deeply analogous to a sign of life on a human face. Facial expressions can flash and ripple; inside a conversation their timing is everything. If you're not paying attention, you can cut yourself off from their resonance. In all three cites, Wittgenstein follows up the rabbit with a person who does not recognize a smile. "If someone sees a smile and does not know it for a smile, does he see it differently from someone who understands it?" Maybe he can say a whole lot about the expression but, like the hare, his description will leave him cold. Of course there are all kinds of people who find Wittgenstein's conversational ideals repugnant. For them joining his circle of the human form of life is like passing through the eye of a needle. Elizabeth Bowen renders this aversion for a couple of chilly members of the British upper class at the culmination of her great novel, *The Death of the Heart,* "If one thought what everyone felt, one would go mad. It does not do to think of what people feel." I refer to Wittgenstein's ideals as a circle of living conversation, because if one assembles his hints and insights into good talk, he compares it to dancing. Here are a couple of pearls from his *Remarks on the Philosophy of Psychology,* Volume I: "Verbal language contains a strong musical element. (A sigh, the modulation of tone for a question, for an announcement, for longing; all the countless *gestures* in the vocal cadences)." "For can anything be more remarkable than this, that the *rhythm* of a sentence should be important for exact understanding of it?"

I would like to end this chapter with an ersatz nod to empiricism: an introspective experiment. Every exclamation carries excitement with it. *Fowler's Modern English Usage* talks about the exclamation point adding "a dash of sensation." Try enclosing other animals in the ". . . !" form. Exclaim them to yourself: "Robin!", "Goat!", "Woodchuck!", "Squirrel!", "Catamount!", "Deer!", "Coyote!", "Snake!", "Rabbit!". They all wear their exclamation points differently. Excitement has for each of them a different sound-shape. Which one is closest to a concrete instance of life as we find it for ourselves?

My answer to this question is Brer Rabbit.

VI

THE RABBIT EVANGELS
Joel Chandler Harris and Beatrix Potter

The complicated structure of words (including stories) and pictures (including memories) that comprise the rabbit between us actually has a discoverable genealogy. Over fifty years ago Bugs Bunny split the family down the middle. Our side includes Peter Rabbit, Peter Cottontail, Uncle Wiggily, the Velveteen Rabbit, Harvey, and Esterhazy. It has more in common with "dust bunnies" (their happenstance, their materialization out of nowhere) than with Bugs and his maniacal descendants (such as Roger Rabbit). Sometime in the early forties Bugs got rid of his rounded look, stood upright, and started acting like a rabbit full of self-confidence, a super rabbit. During the Second World War he developed a Brooklyn accent. At the head of the whole family is Brer Rabbit, the creation of African American folklore. Thanks to Joel Chandler Harris, who spent the best times of his youth in slave cabins, we possess an enormous volume of tales. Beatrix Potter read Harris's early books and made herself into the Aesop of the nursery. (She had already read *Uncle Tom's Cabin*.) This means that we took to a creature who was twice-over a response to oppression, a spiritual liberator: first, the oppression of slavery in the American South; and second, the oppression of childhood in the late Victorian era. Potter not only read Harris's first Uncle Remus book, *Uncle Remus: His Songs and Sayings,* but in the year that she composed the illustrated letter that eventually turned into *The Tale of Peter Rabbit,* she started a series of illustrations for the Uncle Remus stories, which she worked on for the next three years. In the words of Potter's most recent biographer, "*Uncle Remus* was her reference point in the creation of a world where animals and humans overlap." The Brer Rabbit stories sold well, giving rise to a new generation of children's fabulists: Kenneth Grahame (*The Wind in the Willows*), A. A. Milne (*Winnie the Pooh*), Howard Garis (*Uncle Wiggily*), and Thornton Burgess (*Peter Cottontail*). Rudyard Kipling was a great fan of Harris and wrote to him that the tales "ran like wild fire through an English public school. . . . We found ourselves quoting whole pages of Uncle Remus that had got mixed in with the fabric of the old school life."

The politics surrounding Harris and his *Tales of Uncle Remus* are thornier than they have ever been. His books have been removed from bookstores in the name of political correctness—I'm sure he's still sold in Georgia. The principal objections to the *Tales* are that they are written in dialect (with a few stretches in Gullah, the tales told by African Jack), the character of Uncle Remus, and the way the tales are framed. They are told by a freed slave to the little white nephew of his former master, "Mars Jeem". The latter supports Alice Walker's accusation that Harris stole her heritage by making it embarrassing. In the words of Augusta Baker, a prominent Black librarian, as a young girl the dialect struck her like "a foreign language" which she "could not handle." Then, too, the offensive word "nigger" appears throughout. Page duBois writes that "garbled forms of high diction mark Harris's texts." William J. Faulkner, from South Carolina and not Mississippi, translated the tales he grew up on from Simon Brown's Gullah, which he referred to as broken English, into a more standard form. Despite feeling something was lost, he was opposed to "allowing children, black or white, to use dialectal speech in school." All this has led to a rewrite and heavy editing of the tales by a Black author, Julius Lester, in a dialect he describes as "modified contemporary southern black English." Gone as well is the complex character of Uncle Remus, replaced in Lester's version with "a voice," so as to make the tales more "accessible" (which includes less offensive). What Lester has done, it seems to me, is to work a typical piece of information-age voodoo in which actions undertaken in the name of the free, abstract holy grail of "content" push aside the actual medium of creation—in this case, oral culture. Lester's real goal is *readability*, a much more deracinating ambition than the inoffensive-sounding "accessibility."

What's wrong with Uncle Remus? His detractors do not seem to have spent very much time with him. Is it that he tells stories to a white boy? If that's the problem they should be bringing posthumous cases against Old Harbert and George Terrell, who had great affection for Harris when he worked at Turnwold plantation. Jacqueline Shachter, an education professor at Temple University, told the UPI "Uncle Remus was a servile, groveling old 'Uncle Tom'" and went on to accuse Harris of having a "Confederate mentality." According to Walter Brasch, who knows as much about Harris as anyone, in direct conflict with Henry

Grady, chief ideologue of the New South, "Harris, although believing in segregation, hoped it would one day end; he called for a repeal of Jim Crow laws, once writing that the role of a journalist is to '[mow] down the old prejudices that rattle in the wind like weeds.'" R. Bruce Bickley quotes Harris as writing in 1877 that "even the bare suggestion of [slavery's] reestablishment is unsavory." William J. Faulkner called Uncle Remus "an engaging but ignorant and obsequious old black man."

Uncle Remus does not grovel and is not obsequious. He makes it clear to his former masters that he knows more about nature and raising children than they do. As for the charge of "ignorance," let's hear directly from Uncle Remus himself. "I notices dat dem folks w'at makes a great 'miration 'bout w'at dey knows is de folks w'ich you can't put no 'pennunce in w'en de 'cashun come up." This makes for an astonishing conclusion to a remark made by Wittgenstein, "Knowledge, opinion, have no facial expression. There is a tone, a gesture of conviction all right, but only if something is said in this tone, or with this gesture." Before hearing from the great Albert Murray, I want to go on record as claiming that we have more to learn from Uncle Remus than any fictional creation of nineteenth-century America, more than Ahab, Hester Prynne, Inspector Dupin, or Huckleberry Finn. Albert Murray, who obviously knew Harris's tales well, was comfortable calling any older Black man who taught him about life "Uncle Remus"—he once referred to Duke Ellington that way. "Indeed you could point out that so far as you personally were concerned it was Uncle . . . Remus, not Henry James, who first said: "*Boy, keep your eyes and ears open. Boy, try to be one on whom nothing is lost.*"

I am tired of Joel Chandler Harris being disrespected. As a diminutive, red-haired, freckled-face son of an unmarried seamstress who concealed the father's name, he took a lot of abuse from his peers in Eatonton, Georgia. He became pathologically shy and developed a lifelong stammer. When Joel failed to show up at some prescribed time, people knew he could be found sitting on the porch of a slave cabin listening to an older man or woman telling a "legendary tale of [their] race." He wrote in his autobiographical *On the Plantation* that "especially when he was feeling lonely and homesick," he would go sit with Old Harbert and Aunt Crissy (the prototype for Aunt Tempy). As an orphan, I can verify that you don't need a home to feel homesick. Harris discovered African American warmth and kindness; it raised him and he never betrayed it. He was fortunate in the way of white people who overheard slaves singing during Sunday services "breaking out in a torrent of sacred harmony, enough to bear away the whole congregation to heaven." Among the slaves, the Kingdom of God was at hand. Harris trusted Black people enough to be able to tell the Tar Baby story to a large group of railroad workers sitting at night around the train platform of the station at Norcross, Georgia. He "sat next to one of the liveliest talkers in the party. . . . The story was told in a low tone, as if to avoid attracting attention, but the comments of the negro, who was a little past middle age, were loud and frequent. 'Dar now!' he would exclaim, or 'He's a honey, Mon!' or 'Gentermens! git out the way, an' gin 'im room!'" Harris once told his publisher, Walter Hines Page, that he could "*think* in the negro dialect" and that he could translate Ralph Waldo Emerson into it just as well as he could tell the adventures of Brer Rabbit. Robert Cochran in *African American Review* quotes Harris as claiming that his "nostalgia was more for a black world than a white one." When Harris took up his pen he became an "other fellow." According to Cochran, it was as Uncle Remus's "son" that he found his freedom and his voice. When he didn't have a pen in his hand Harris had to pass for white, an identity which dogged him until the end of his life. Imagine what he could hear in the dialect he grew up on—a whole culture. This is what's wrong with Roger Abrahams' modifications of the Uncle Remus tales:

> We simply cannot get beyond the racist resonances that the Uncle Remus–style tellings continue to carry, precisely because the stories are rendered in the dialects of slavery times. I have attempted to take some of this stigma away by using contemporary spellings, and by changing some of the vernacular turns of phrase that would have been familiar to the nineteenth-century reader but have been lost in their currency—and thus their pungency—today.

Abrahams is making a concession to racism; the stigma is on him because of his refrigerator language. When is America going to wake up to the fact that some of the highest levels of humanity attained in this country were achieved by the slaves—and connected to that they gave us music to live by? Their language should be taught in schools so our children can learn, as James Whitcomb Riley (a friend of Harris) put it, "the inner characteristic of the people whose . . . native tongue it is." Riley goes on to say very accurately that the dialect in the tales conveys to us "a positive force of soul, truth, dignity, beauty, grace, purity, and sweetness, that can touch us to the tenderness of tears." I think the lessons it took classicists so agonizingly long to learn about the oral basis of Homeric culture are holding back contemporary scholars from establishing the meaning of the fact that the great body of Black folklore was created by the slaves. When Uncle Remus speaks dialect, often what appears on the page are not words we *read* but a picket fence of letters we must *sound out* in order to get through to the experiences on the other side. Who wants to lose words like "projicky," "pirootin'," "'havishness," "segashuate" or "roach"; or idioms like "bang my times," "dry grins," or "des ez big ez life un twice ez nat'al"; or proverbs such as "He des lay dar des ez ca'm ez a dead pig in de sunshine," "You marry en den you er des lak Brer Fox wid he bag. You know what you put in it, but you dunner w'at you got in it," or the couplet about Ole Brer Tarrypin, "W'en in he prime/He tuck he time!"

Writing about dialect to the editor of *Scribner's Magazine,* Harris makes a point very similar to Wittgenstein's in the last chapter between someone who recognizes a rabbit and someone who does not. "[D]ialect . . . gives a new coloring to statement, and allows of swift shading in narrative that can be reached in literary English only in the most painful and roundabout way. . . . In all dialects the thought exactly fits the expression—the idea is as homely as the words—and any attempt to reproduce dialect must recognize this fact or be pronounced a failure." In another context, speaking about interpretation, Wittgenstein matches Harris's thought teetotal. "The question whether what is involved is a seeing or an act of interpreting arises because an interpretation becomes an expression of experience. And the interpretation is not an indirect description; no, it is the primary expression of the experience."

I would like to end the Harris section by proposing yet one more motto for America. It's from Jean Toomer's *Cane*: "The Dixie Pike has grown from a goat path in Africa."

Had the near-contradictory concept of "benign neglect" ever admitted of legal prosecution, Beatrix Potter's childhood could well have served as Exhibit A. Not only did her wealthy parents have precious little to do with her: they left her in the perpetual care of nursemaids and governesses and mostly unsent for on the third floor of their Kensington mansion—Bolton Gardens —which an irreverent cousin described as a "dark Victorian mausoleum complete with aspidistras." They also seem to have made no provisions for her eventual entry into the outside world, for her exiting the "family programme" as she called it. A kind of latchkey child in reverse, they hardly introduced her to anybody. Her father, who had indeed fostered her artistic pursuits, failed to acquaint her with any of his friends when as a young woman she accompanied him on visits to various art exhibitions, which had the predictable effect of making her wonder if he was ashamed of her. As she wrote in her journal (in code that took years to decipher after her death), "I always thought I was born to be a discredit to my parents." Nothing that I have read directly addresses the question of what her parents were thinking. My guess is that we are looking at the void created by two ardent social climbers from the upper middle class who, having maxed out their social connections, *preferred to dream* about their daughter's marriage prospects. Rather than actually presenting her and having to admit that they were not going to break into the upper crust, they seem to have indulged the fantasy that some Peter Pan from the upper class might fly into the third-floor nursery and marry her. (By the way, Potter's most recent biographer, Linda Lear, denies what her first biographer, Margaret Lane, asserts, namely, that there were bars on the windows of the nursery—either way, Beatrix was a prisoner.)

Inside this cloistered existence Beatrix, along with her younger brother, managed to work out an amazing childhood vocation such that in retrospect she could say she was glad she had never been sent to school because it would have "rubbed off some of the originality (if I had not died of shyness or been killed with over pressure)." Lane makes the astute observation that, "Beatrix had always, from her earliest years, had a strong sense of the unreality of Bolton Gardens, servants, formality, 'manners,' routine . . ."—as we might put it, she found the symbolism repellent. Real life for Beatrix is what she found during her summer vacations in the Border Country of Scotland when she was allowed to wander, by herself it seems, in nearby fields and farmyards. This was the point of origin of Beatrix's genius, rendered by Lane with the utmost lucidity:

> Everything that she saw was suddenly "real." Farms and cottages were real. Animals were real. Even the frog captured for a moment among the stones of a stream or the wood-mouse washing its whiskers under a leaf, led interesting and reasonable lives according to their conditions. They were beautiful to look at, too; mysterious, full of surprises, intent on their small concerns with a completeness which allowed her, crouched in a trance of stillness among the ferns, to share their lives for the space of long summer afternoons, and to understand, as a child's

imagination can, what it feels like to thread one's way under the grass and bracken. This vision of the beauty and integrity of wild life, on however tiny a scale, was peculiarly clear, and still kept its freshness and innocence of eye as she grew older.

This marked the beginning of what became a truly incredible period of years devoted to studying and living with all kinds of little animals, along with plants and insects. She and her brother collected everything they could find and smuggled a lot of it into their quarters: beetles, toadstools, minnows, hedgehogs, frogs, caterpillars, dead birds, sloughed snakeskins. . . . They would skin dead specimens or, if they were too far gone, boil them and collect the bones. They once did this with a dead fox and succeeded in reassembling the entire skeleton. Back home in Bolton Gardens, Beatrix drew and painted pressed flowers she brought home from the country in blotting paper (from her earliest years she took to paint-box and pencil and had long been given to copying plates of animals and birds from natural history books). She studied the skeletons of field mice, raised a family of snails and *kept a journal of their lives*! Soon the real menagerie started to materialize. First two field mice were sneaked in, in a box. Then came a rabbit who was supposed to be staying in a hutch in the back gardens, "but was generally stretched in civilized ease on the hearth rug"—rabbits are known to like to stretch out on their sides and bask, eyes closed, in the sun. There were pet bats who spent the day hanging upside down in a parrot's cage, but at dusk would commence to zig-zag around the room, eventually coming to roost on her fingers. She also had a pet hedgehog named Tiggy who drank out of a doll-sized teacup.

This arrangement, a very imaginative solitude created out of distance from her patter-rolling parents, seems to have worked for Beatrix until she was sixteen, when she began to feel "the peaceful time of childhood was ending" and foresaw changes in her life. It was at this time that she began her secret journal in cipher that ran to over 200,000 words, continued until she was near thirty. (The engineer, Leslie Linder, who spent over six years of his spare time before he eventually broke her code, wrote about the additional difficulties due to her invented script-characters being "so small—*so* small—they looked as though they had been made by little mice.") I should add that her use of code was the first of a few things about her that put me in mind of Samuel Beckett, whom I have always believed took to writing French in order to shield his prose from the imagined intrusions of his mother. Another is Beatrix's description of her writing method, essentially subtraction: "My usual way of writing is to scribble and cut out, and write it again and again. The shorter and plainer the better." I won't say she had Beckett's eyes. She had the most absorbent eyes I have ever seen. Her eyes defy Wittgenstein's phenomenology of the eye, but Beckett's satisfy it. "We don't see the human eye as a receiver; it seems, not to let something in, but to send out. The ear receives; the eye looks. (It casts glances, it flashes, beams, coruscates.)" Sixteen seems to have been the age when the receptivity of her eyes first surfaced and took permanent possession of her face. Lane records a wonderful description of her silent, disconcerting stare, "the searching, expressionless stare of a little animal."

Lane also brought a highly poetic term to bear on Beatrix's demeanor: *farouche*. The entry in Webster's dictionary under this word will take us from the dead-on stare of her adolescent photograph, clear back to her hands and knees exploration of the Border Country: "farouche *adj.* [French. wild, shy, from Late Latin *forasticus* living outside, fr. Latin *foras* outdoors; akin to Latin *fores* door—more at DOOR] 1. WILD 2: marked by shyness and lack of social graces." At sixteen Beatrix could not "see"—that is, project—a future. She found herself face to face with the right-hand side of a temporal parenthesis (a suspension) that continued to open up behind her. She wrote in her journal on New Year's Eve 1885, "How awful it seems at the end of a year to think it has actually passed into space never to return! Gone except its memories! Much bitterness and a few peaceful summer days. Oh life, wearisome, disappointing, and yet in many shades so sweet, I wonder why one is so unwilling to let go this old year? not because it has been joyful, but because I fear its successors—I am terribly afraid of the future. Some fears will inevitably be fulfilled, and the rest is dark—Peace to the old year, may the seed sown therein be no bitter fruit." She also now began to suffer chronic depression—"bad times" as she called them—with the usual low spirits, generalized fatigue, and various rheumatic-style symptoms. Beatrix was actually in a fantastic temporal trap the like of which I have never seen or heard tell. On the front side was the dead wall of the future invigilated by her parents well into her thirties. (At age thirty-six, for example, they would not allow her to visit the offices of her publisher without a chaperone.) Here we might ponder out a comparison between Joel Chandler Harris's masquerade as a Southerner and Beatrix Potter's thoroughgoing imitation of daughterly piety. In private she referred to her mother as "the enemy," but never challenged her parents' right to dictate to her on social matters. They both discoursed with slaves—Potter read Uncle Remus. (It was probably the little animals that they identified with that opened up the histrionic space in their lives.) Behind her was a past that was as open and transparent to her as the future was closed and opaque. Beatrix seems to have been one of those rare individuals who was spared the moral catastrophe of childhood amnesia. Maybe the little animals kept the backward path clear of obstructions. "I have been laughed at for what I say I can remember; but it is admitted that I can remember quite plainly from one and two years old; not only facts like learning to walk, but places and sentiments—the way things impressed a very young child." After she finally married, she could in truth declare, "the child in me lived on, concealed, until I was fifty."

Childhood amnesia is a moral catastrophe because it is the main reason we make the wrong thing out of our childhood and thus one big reason we make the wrong self. With childhood amnesia something definitive—on the order of a shock—interrupts the flow of life and establishes itself as the new outer limit of "continuous memory" (actually just beyond the outer limit); while earlier events are now completely forgotten (suppressed) or dragged along as meaningless fragments that magnetize corresponding events. My own continuous memory begins at roughly three and a half with my face pressed against the windowpane, watching the snow accumulate on Lafayette Avenue. This was after a series of denied transfers from a home for unwed mothers to my adoptive parents, to my adoptive grandmother for six months who restored me to good health, and then back to my adoptive parents for a year and a half in an apartment that was never referred to again. Something happened to me when I saw the movie *Alice Doesn't Live Here Anymore*. I think the title of the movie primed me and I became haunted by the little girl playing "Where or When" on the piano in a house alone. This would be about my grandmother. Before that episode I used to hear the song "Secret Love" as religious.

Despite all this I continue to be amazed at story after story about children who were adopted at six, seven, or eight years old and do not know that they were adopted because they do not remember back that far. After driving across the country together, you yourself formed the impression that your sister had forgotten large portions of her childhood. I can support that judgment because I noticed that after she left for college, Margie was not at all given to reminiscence—she seemed to refuse to let memories move her. After we lost the court case, she had no hopes of getting to the yonder side of her mother.

What was Beatrix to do? Childhood (now for her an internal possession) was over and the future completely occluded. In 1883 her parents took her to the Winter Exhibition of Old Masters at the Royal Academy, where she had a genuinely oracular experience—communicated only to her journal. While her favorite painting was a portrait by Titian (*Caterina Cornaro, Queen of Cyprus*), what really seems to have gotten into her was a work, entitled *Design,* by Angelica Kauffmann: "That picture . . . is something, it shows what a woman has done." In the same entry she described Kauffmann's drawing as "bold and firm, the arms and hands being particularly striking. *I seemed to see the hands move*" (emphasis added). Seven weeks later, she wrote the following sentence in her journal: "I *will* do something sooner or later." By moving her own hands, Beatrix not only fought off depression, but by a sequence that seems, once you know it, divinely inspired, she eventually broke up the stasis of her life and produced a rabbit that made her enough money to buy her way out of Bolton Gardens and secure the independence of which she had always dreamt.

Without in any way wishing to minimize her absolute heroism—the illnesses, the suffering, the setbacks, the continued interference and hypercriticism from her parents—I would like to set out in rather schematic fashion the elements and steps by which Beatrix hacked through the Gordian knot of her life.

(i) *Drawing and Depression*: Without calling her a graphomaniac (which sounds too pathological), Beatrix did, indeed, feel a compulsion to draw, which evidently could intrude on social occasions—like dinner parties. But then again we know she was shy. What was the real secret behind the urge to draw and the curative powers it had for her? She gives it away in a journal passage:

> the irresistible desire to copy any beautiful object which strikes the eye. Why cannot one be content to look at it? I cannot rest, I *must* draw, however poor the result, and when I have a bad time come over me it is a stronger desire than ever, and settles on the queerest thing, worse than queer sometimes. Last time, in the middle of September, I caught myself in the back yard making a careful and admiring copy of the swill bucket, and the laugh it gave me brought me round.

Beatrix seems not to have been able to *talk* for any length of time about herself, her work, her tastes, her familiars without using words like "trash" or "rubbish" (e.g. "I can manage to describe little rubbish like mice and rabbits.") She found beautiful anything she was allied with. Here one simply has to ask what could be more like a depressed person than a swill bucket? For Beatrix, the road out of depression involved her bestowing acts of loving attention—drawing, not British speech because her mother was too exacting—on the contemptible objects she identified with. Anyone who has suffered depression knows that more direct acts of self-appreciation are out of the question. Beatrix was certainly not going to raise her spirits by doing a self-portrait in the mirror, because she was certain that her face had been "spoiled" by the length of her nose and upper lip. (There is knowledge for you.) Circuitousness is the rule.

(ii) *Fossils*: If we were to imagine the passion of Beatrix Potter as a series of sculpted panels, I would place the Illusion of Moving Hands in the prologue position. Then the swill bucket. Immediately after that comes a relief of Beatrix bent over a fossil case at the Kensington Museum, drawing. Beatrix had picked up the then-fashionable interest in geology. She pursued it obsessively and secretly in her journals; but the drawing was out in the open, even public. Even after fossils had been displaced from the center of her attention, she continued to draw them because they had a restorative effect. What was truly kinetic about these outings is that she put herself in effective correspondence with the figure—a marble torso—in the Angelica Kauffmann painting. Both are liberating—something living that has been captured in stone. With regard to Beatrix, we're talking about a delicate form of life negatively embedded in the volcanic rock of her parents. A certain kind of person gets interested in geology because of its stunning ability to replace nouns like "fossil" with verbs like "fossilize," to discover that the given is *in processu*. But the drawing of fossils was not just a figurative expression of "geologic" hope. It was a genuine step forward because, unlike the swill bucket, the fossil is a metaphorically accurate rendering of her predicament. Maybe she felt comfortable enough with the word "fossil" to stand under it like a marquee. Perhaps it unraveled some of the tension with her parents.

(iii) *Fungus*: "Now of all the hopeless things to draw, I should think that the very worst is a fine fat fungus." But for the existence of a misogynist layer at the directorship of the Royal Botanical Gardens, Beatrix Potter might have become famous for what would have been a beautifully illustrated book on mycology. On her own she arrived at the conclusion, contrary to current scientific opinion, that lichens were dual organisms, funguses living symbiotically with algae. Her work, which was later vindicated, was rejected out of hand. It is tempting to see her discovery here as a charmed extension of another symbiosis of which she had long been apprised: that between funguses and fairies. When she was thirty years old, she could describe as one of her pleasantest memories in the Lake District, a Sunday afternoon sitting with her legs dangling over a rock ledge listening to:

> all the little tiny fungus people singing and bobbing and dancing in the grass and under the leaves all down below, like the whistling that some people cannot hear of stray

mice and bats, and I sitting above and knowing something about them.

I cannot tell what possesses me with the fancy that
they laugh and clap their hands, especially the little ones
that grow in troops and rings amongst the dead leaves
in the woods. I suppose it is the fairy rings, the myriads
of fairy fungi that start to life in autumn woods.

I remember I used to half believe and wholly play
with fairies when I was a child. What heaven can be more
real than to retain the spirit-world of childhood, tem-
pered and balanced by knowledge and common sense,
to fear no longer the terror that flieth by night, yet to feel
truly and understand a little, a very little, of the story of
life.

One thing that stands out in so many of her mentions of
fairies is that Beatrix will locate herself *right next to them*. When
it comes to fairies I am really out of my depth. I only learned
about them through *A Midsummer Night's Dream*. There I
learned that Oberon and Titania are the king and queen of fairies
in Britain; that Robin Goodfellow, alias Puck, could put a girdle
round the earth in forty minutes; that "fairy time" is bedtime;
and that fairies have a lot to do with love. Do fairies and funguses darkle—grow in the dark? The few paintings she did of
funguses that I have seen are truly gorgeous and, importantly,
she shared the quest for rare fungus with a specific individual.
Charlie McIntosh was an older rural postman, who like Beatrix
was both shy and a learned and self-taught naturalist. When they
finally discussed funguses "he became quite excited and spoke
with quite poetical feeling about their exquisite colours." Beatrix

herself had exquisite colour. Next comes the passage about the "hopeless things to draw . . . the very worst a fine fat fungus." After that she writes, "I happened by lucky intuition to have drawn several rare species. One with white spikes on the lower side he had discovered this summer for the first time in a wood at Murthly, and another, like a spluttered candle."

The last phrase comes from an Uncle Remus story, "Why Brother Wolf Didn't Eat the Little Rabbits." He has fallen asleep in a chair in the little boy's room and Miss Sally roused him by tapping with her thimble on his bald spot. When he woke up "de clock wuz a-clockin' en de candle a-splutterin.'" I think we can hear Beatrix talking about herself here and it's getting late in the game. It was autumn, and about autumn she wrote near the end of her journal, "The autumn is a time that makes one think there is no time like the present, and the present is very pleasant." Maybe she felt like a bit of fall foliage covering up fungus and fairies, but at least she was in positive *dialogue* about her qualities.

(iv) *Illustrated Letters to Children*: ["Here comes the rabbit, . . . rabbit, . . . rabbit"—dog-racing announcement.] Beatrix began to lay the groundwork for *The Tale of Peter Rabbit* well before her life with fungus and Charlie McIntosh got underway. In February 1890, she began to write letters in her journal to an imaginary friend named Esther, "in humble imitation of my heroine Fanny Burney," whose early diaries had been addressed to her younger sister Esther and recently been republished. In her second letter to Esther, Beatrix repudiates the mumbo jumbo she's up to (magic "that makes the troubled spirits of ancestors go away") by using the Latin phrase *"absit omen"* ("let there be no omen") in her first sentence. The week of her first letter to Esther was also the week she began privately to prepare six designs for Christmas cards, all featuring her pet rabbit, Benjamin Bouncer, as a model. The "root" of this happy business was "pique [i.e. transiently wounded vanity] and a desire for coin to the amount of £6." Her elated second letter to Esther was written after receiving a cheque for £6 from the firm of Hildesheimer & Faulkner. She makes a cryptic pun at the beginning of the letter; she disavows the "coincidence" between beginning to write to Esther and coin falling from heaven into her life. This letter also contains a description of her celebration with Benjamin Bouncer up in her quarters.

We have here two elements that, finally conjoined, will produce the famous Beatrix Potter. Her journal has undergone a discourse adjustment. She has admitted into the inert solitude of "no-one-will-read-this" an imaginary interlocutor whose effect is to sprinkle the germ of movement into her prose and get things going off the page. Something is stirring. Utterly important is the fact that her imaginary addressee is a younger person. Beatrix will not be opening herself up to examination by adults. A second important element is the rabbit factor. Beatrix loved all kinds of little animals: her pet mouse, Hunca Munca; her green lizard, Judy; and Tiggy the hedgehog. Nonetheless, it seems a foregone conclusion that Beatrix would venture into the world behind a rabbit. Brer Rabbit was a literary star in England. Favorite or no, she was clearly closer to and more involved with her pet "jack hare" than any other animal in her menagerie. Beatrix and Benjamin Bouncer were valenced companions; they teamed up like Aphrodite and Eros. Eros, the constant companion of

Aphrodite, is about as close as the Greeks ever came to Brer Rabbit. Not only was he a notorious trickster, but his parentage (according to Socrates' tutor, Diotima) *Penia* (poverty) and *Poros* (the way through) puts one in mind of Brer Rabbit's general circumstance. The fact is that she and Bounce were pretty far along in the process the Stoics called *oikeiosis,* the process of coming to belong together. The night the cheque arrived,

> My first act was to give Bounce . . . a cupful of hemp seeds, the consequence being that when I wanted to draw him next morning he was partially intoxicated and wholly unmanageable.

> Then I retired to bed, and lay chuckling till 2 in the morning, and afterwards had the impression that Bunny came to my bedside in a white cotton night cap and tickled me with his whiskers.

Another journal entry will enable us to ask a properly symmetrical question: "Which dreamed it?" One night in Scotland, having rescued a raggedy female rabbit from a snare (much to her father's indignation) Beatrix confided,

> I just had enough sense not to show the stranger to Benjamin Bounce, but the smell of its fur on my dress was quite enough to upset the ill-regulated passions of that excitable buck rabbit. . . .

> Whether he thought I had a rival in my pocket, or like a Princess in a Fairy Tale was myself metamorphosed into a white rabbit I cannot say, but I had to lock him up.

In this suit, Potter v. Bounce, we would do well to judge like Solomon and award them joint custody of the dream. In the meantime we find ourselves once again at the barrier between humans and animals; and lo and behold there is traffic there. Just like at the very beginning when I had the riveting experience of being unable to properly separate you from the little rabbit on the postcard. I tried to spread my discomfort about this by arguing that the fictional membrane around Kafka's *Metamorphosis* is not intact. We have just heard hints of a couple of breaches. Throughout this piece about the descent of the spirit of the rabbit onto us, we have never strayed far from the wizardry known to the slaves as "conjure." Eric Sundquist defines the conjurer as someone "who had the power to charm or curse or heal individuals . . . by the use of bags or balls filled with secret ingredients, . . . by using roots or animal parts made into a potion or poison." They could change people into animals. Sundquist adds that "those slaves or free blacks who did not believe in conjure—Frederick Douglass and Martin Delany, to cite two examples—might also dismiss it as a psychological game practiced on the ignorant and gullible." The problem is that none of us know how ignorant or gullible we are. Conjure appears to be outside the circle of believability. We presume that humans do not change into animals; that there are no werewolves; and that at most Beatrix and Benjamin were dreaming. Conjure is not for people who live like us; it is not even on the outskirts of religious belief. Yet I have to tell you of a bracing episode in which a case of conjure turned up right in the middle of my living room. The fact that it maintained conjure-status only for a minute or so has done nothing to remove the epistemic stain for the moment I believed.

The event in question took place when Lynn, myself, and Widdershins (she liked the pun-quality of the word, she was left-handed, and enjoyed going against the grain) were sharing a brick duplex on Potomac Avenue in Buffalo. I was eating dinner in front of the television with Widdershins. Lynn was toiling two rooms away in the TV-proof kitchen. (She disliked TV and saw it as a way to fix you to the house.) We were watching a soap opera in Spanish, *El Premio Major,* which neither of us understood. How stupid! We were getting comfortable with not appreciating what people said. Just about the time when dinner and the show were winding down, a very large German shepherd wearing a red bandana around its neck came loping out of the kitchen, through the dining room and into the living room. More than frightened, because I had never seen this dog before, I went to the kitchen and found no Lynn and the door to the back stairway closed. Both of us, Widdershins and myself, sank into the conjure moment: Lynn had transmogrified into a German shepherd. Anyone who knew Lynn at the time knew of her feeling for dogs, her admiration for their nature, and her deep determination to defend their intellect and powers of communication against the philosophical slanders that had long been carrying the day. As much as anything—more than the closed door—the bandana was the clinching detail. It bore a disconcertingly close resemblance in color and pattern to the item Lynn had been tying around her waist and using as (her mother's term) a "tail." Of course things were quite otherwise and I will not bother you with the specifics of how the truth sorted itself back to normal a few minutes later. Nothing changes the fact that a crazy belief managed to set itself up for a minute or so before disappearing.

Conjure dates from a time and culture in which buildings had not yet displaced animals in the human psyche. This time happens to coincide with the condition of humans being supremely important to one another. In my limited research into the question of "belief," I found that the concept originates in trust of another human being, and does not achieve the familiar form until one or another dogmatic regime of propositions opposes itself to the order of magic, driving magic and the supremacy of human relations underground. In his criticism of Frazer's *Golden Bough*, Wittgenstein states that "men (spirits) can be dangerous to a man and everyone knows this." These latter relations will always hollow out large areas inside the web of knowledge, making for the ever-present possibility of collapses.

It so happens that at the time of Lynn's supposed transformation, Widdershins' secret intention was to slip into Lynn's spirit like a garment. She attempted to expropriate for herself the whole realm of Lynn's self-expression. I didn't realize the lengths she went to simulate Lynn, and I never learned what it was like to have so much of oneself played back element by element in a serious but degraded form by someone across from you. I admit as somebody who grew up on lies, I tried to smooth things over and indulged the awful habit of finishing Widdershins' sentences for her. I succumbed to the alibi of imitation's flattery and failed to be suspicious of her garbled speech. I also did not make anything out of the fact she was reading and enjoying Dostoyevksy's nightmarishly difficult novella *The Double*, where a clerk is being driven mad by a mysterious apparition of himself, a second Golyadkin. I found the story impossible to read.

So for a moment Widdershins and I fell guiltily through the floor on which we were dancing our *folie circulaire* and landed in the underground river of conjure. Lynn had changed into an animal (as is often the case with conjuring) to get to another life. I fell down like a building when a lawyer told me two months later that I was adopted.

Back to Beatrix. To gather from her journals, one of the principal and most lovable functions of rabbits in general, and Bounce in particular, is to *upset the family equation*, to tilt it by a few shades of meaning toward Beatrix. Surely the following little anecdote is meant to be pinned onto her father, with the further implication that Beatrix herself is a lineal rabbit. "I read a story once that a certain arab setting eyes for the first time on an ass, exclaimed, 'behold the father of all hares.'" Earlier in her journal she reports that Benjamin Bunny once travelled in a covered basket and when she took him out, he "proved scared and bit the family." In the same entry she records his "funniest exploit," he happened to be in High Street with the family butler, "Cox, when, seeing a footman throw open the door of a carriage, he jumped in with great presence of mind in front of some ladies." I cannot help but hear in those vignettes the proleptic thought that someday a rabbit running well ahead of Beatrix's mother will outmaneuver her in the matter of finding a husband.

At the same time, however, the Potter family equation was being seriously eroded by a Black Uncle and a "black rabbit" (cf. *Mr. Tod* and *Apply Dapply's Nursery Rhymes*): Uncle Remus and Brer Rabbit. After the Christmas card success, Beatrix started giving serious thought to becoming a book illustrator, and early in 1893 began a mystical apprenticeship the nature of which—while leaving plenty of clues—she kept secret her entire life. She commenced work that would continue for a number of years on a series of drawings (eight in all) for the Uncle Remus tales to which she was clearly devoted. In a wonderful piece of detective work, John Goldthwaite asks in *The Natural History of Make-Believe* why she picked the story, "Mr. Wolf Makes a Failure," to illustrate before any other. The answer is to be found in how the story begins:

> "I lay yo' ma got company," said Uncle Remus, as the little boy entered the old man's door with a huge piece of mince-pie in his hand, "en ef she ain't got comp'ny, den she done gone en drap de cubberd key somers whar you done run up wid it."
>
> "Well, I saw the pie lying there, Uncle Remus, and I just thought I'd fetch it out to you."
>
> "Tooby sho, honey," replied the old man, regarding the child with admiration. "Tooby sho, honey; dat changes marters."

As Goldthwaite observes, this "marks the first time in the series that the little boy appears at Uncle Remus's door because his parents are too busy for him. As we know too well, Potter's own parents shared virtually nothing with their daughter. . . . Never did they regard her with the admiration Uncle Remus bestows on the little boy. There was never a moment like this in her life." We are back at the site of the dream that Joel Chandler Harris refused to renounce, that of a childhood in a Black world. Uncle Remus consistently claims and demonstrates that he possesses knowledge superior to that of genteel whites about things that count, namely, about the right way to raise children and the workings of nature. One feels this all the way through the tales. Beatrix stayed clandestine about her connections to Uncle Remus because she was secretly switching families and on the way to becoming a trixter herself. Very supple.

Interestingly enough, we know the very day she turned Peter Rabbit loose. Perhaps just as interesting, we know what she did the day before (she imagined herself to be Brer Rabbit's accomplice in a garden her father was renting). On September 4, 1893, she wrote an illustrated letter to five-year-old Noel Moore, the son of her former governess, who was sick in bed. The letter began, "I don't know what to write to you, so I shall tell you a story about four little rabbits whose names were Flopsy, Mopsy, Cottontail and Peter." She had been writing letters with pictures to the Moore children and various young cousins since the spring of the previous year. She wrote about the strange doings of her pets or of animals she had seen in her travels, and also about the foibles of her family. She wrote in a voice that had been evolving in the journals, a voice that Goldthwaite aptly describes as very much like Uncle Remus's in that it is "easy with itself, straightforward, and intimate in its attentiveness to the small things of the moment. It is the voice of someone who is a friend of the hero and a friend of the reader and who is passing on information of interest." He then quotes from the letter to Noel, "I think he [Peter Rabbit] would have got away altogether, if he had not unfortunately run into a gooseberry net and got caught fast by the large buttons of his jacket. It was a blue jacket with brass buttons; quite new."

On the day prior, September 3, she had been painting on site an extremely rare pinecone fungus she had found in the very garden that would double the next day as the location for Peter Rabbit's raid on Mr. McGregor. (The estate where all this took place was sublet to the Potters by one Atholl McGregor.) Her discovery was a kind of climax—or maybe a denouement—to a summer largely spent searching for fungi, often in the company of Charlie McIntosh, and painting. It was also a summer in which her journal went quiet. Given that she abandoned the journal altogether once she started to publish the little books, the summer shut-down tells us that she was brooding the story of Peter Rabbit. Can we make the hypothesis that the books were an extension of the journal by other means? She was about to do something bad (excuse me, mischievous) modeled on the behavior of a young girl who turns up twice—the second time on the threshold of womanhood—in *Uncle Remus* (cf. "Brother Rabbit and the Little Girl" and "In Some Lady's Garden"). She is going to let a stealing little rabbit into her father's garden. Between September 3 and September 4, Beatrix was turning in place. On the 3rd she made a drawing of the newly discovered fungus, on the back of which she sketched McGregor's garden, putting an X on the spot where she had found it. Presumably so Charlie McIntosh might know where it would appear in the future. I find that X a touch provocative. She used the same device (enhanced to an asterisk) some fifteen years later in *The Tale of Samuel Whiskers* to mark the spot on the attic wall behind which her naughty hero of the moment, Tom Kitten, was crawling along in the uncomfortably tight and unrepresentable dark. *Samuel Whiskers* is a lightly encrypted account of how she got rid of her parents by purchasing the farm at Sawry. We need only identify the two protagonist rats, Samuel Whiskers as her father (any photo of Rupert screams out the "whiskers" association) and his shrill and argumentative wife, Anna Maria, as her mother. Near the end of the story, Beatrix, as far as I know for the only time in the Peter Rabbit books, appears as herself, standing at a lane watching the two rats scurry away with their stolen goods.—By the way, the Potters' fortune came from cotton.— Seeing her there, off in the distance, beholding the flight of her parents feels a little miraculous. Do you think she told Charlie McIntosh that she would be using his face on the morrow for the irate Mr. McGregor? I think she handed him a map marking the garden where all the hidden treasure she acquired from Uncle Remus over the previous months was buried. She was about to effect a brilliant translation of creeturtime into the nurseries of England.

VII

OBLITERATURE

One day I was on the phone with your sister Margie when your stepfather got on the line and asked in a very stagey voice, "Do you know who you are? You are Peter Quint! That's who you are." Peter Quint is the dead, former valet in Henry James' *The Turn of the Screw* believed by the current governess to be haunting ("visiting") her little charges, Flora and Miles, along with her dead predecessor, Miss Jessel. Because he was speaking emphatically from a very well-woven text, he told me more about himself than he told me about me. The only one who sees the ghosts of Peter Quint and Miss Jessel in *The Turn of the Screw* is the governess. She sees him as she sees "the letters I form on the page." So I was not being treated as real, but being *read*. In choosing the name Peter Quint, James very deliberately hitched his novella to a play of Shakespeare's. *The Turn of the Screw* floats like a reversal on the lake of *A Midsummer Night's Dream*. In the Preface to the New York Edition, he refers to his story as "a fairy-tale pure and simple," but, differing from Shakespeare's play, it does not spring from "a conscious and cultivated credulity." There are no fairies in the story, but the governess repeatedly describes the children as angels. At one point, she makes an oblique dip into *Midsummer Night's Dream* and declares how the children pop out at her as "Shakespeareans, astronomers and navigators," that is, fairies endowed with the knowledge of the night sky and the ability to circle the earth in a matter of minutes. In the same preface James tells his reader the opposite of what Oberon, the king of the fairies, tells his servant Robin Goodfellow, that "Good ghosts . . . make poor subjects, . . . there would be laid on [Peter Quint and Miss Jessel] the dire duty of causing the situation to reek with an air of Evil; [they] are not 'ghosts' at all . . . but goblins, elves, imps, demons as loosely constructed as those of the old trials for witchcraft." Robin complains to Oberon, "Damned spirits all, / That in crossways and floods have burial, / Already to the wormy beds are gone." Oberon replies, "But we are spirits of another sort. / I with the Morning's love have oft made sport." A pair of contrary premises run through the two stories. In *Midsummer Night* the fairies see to it that all the love in the play culminates in marriage. But the "demons" in the governess's head prevent her from ever marrying her employer, the children's uncle, who "seduced" her. In reckoning with Peter Quint, she cuts short the life of Miles who loved him.

Why does Henry James choose Peter Quince among the Athenian craftsmen who are putting on the play *Pyramus and Thisbe* to celebrate the marriage of Theseus and Hippolyta? As a governess, she can be presumed to know Shakespeare's plays. She actually confides to the housekeeper, Mrs. Grose, who knew Peter Quint, that the phantom in her brain gives her "a sort of sense of looking like an actor." Mrs. Grose turns pale, no one could have resembled an actor less. James picked Quince because the prologue he composes for the beginning of *Pyramus and Thisbe* applies to what the governess is up to, and provokes in her many self-critical ruminations:

> Gentles, perchance you wonder at this show.
> But wonder on, till truth make all things plain.
> This man is Pyramus, if you know.
> This beauteous lady Thisbe is certain.
> This man with lime and rough-cast doth present
> Wall, that vile wall which did these lovers sunder;
> And through Wall's chink, poor souls, they are content
> To whisper, at the which let no man wonder.

The governess describes her mission as that of being a [vile] wall between the children and their former loves. "The children in special I should thus fence about and absolutely save." "I was a screen—I was to stand before them. The more I saw the less they would." "I was like a gaoler with an eye to possible surprises and escapes." She should have remembered the line from *Midsummer Night*, "Love looks not with the eyes but with the mind; / And therefore is winged Cupid painted blind."

When people spontaneously lapse into drama—speak through another character—they have to identify with the person they have become. I have only renounced my identity twice in my life. When I was in grammar school I wanted people to think of me as Mickey Mantle's doppelgänger. I know now that my great affinity for him was based on his carrying painful secrets throughout his life. A decade later, I fell in love with the poet Ed Dorn and occasionally announced myself as him on the phone. What I loved about Ed Dorn was his language. Both of our mothers were descended from Kentucky pioneers. I felt he spoke from the same source as me. He later identified himself as a "lostling." He used to enjoy the pun on the river he grew up next to, the Embarras. I liked the homophonic echo of the state I was born in, the Hoosier State (who's yer mommy? who's yer daddy?). Donald Davie, the English poet, has a beautiful description of Dorn's language: "What validates Dorn's lyric voice is, time and again, its humility, the instruction it looks for and gets from people and places and happenings. It reflects on them, it moralizes on them; but the reflection and the moral are drawn not from some previously accumulated stock of wisdom, but (so the writing persuades us) immediately out of the shock of confronting each of them as it comes, unpredictably."

Can we presume that the governess got under your step-father's skin? Something must have motivated him to blurt out what he said on the phone. Like the governess, he was in receipt of disturbing communications from previous family. He believed of small children that they had "scant enough 'antecedents.'" (He hid from his younger daughter when she visited.) Gathering from his intonation on the phone, he proposed to give one more turn of the screw by means of moral judgment. The phrase is defined explicitly in *What Maisie Knew* by Mrs. Wix. "It would take another turn of the screw to desert" their father. Bottom in *Midsummer Night* opposes the encapsulation of love, he speaks the line, "reason and love keep little company together nowadays."

It was not very long after we lost the court case that another piece of literature, *Gone with the Wind,* came down the road and began to filter your sister's relations to all of us. Margie became one of Margaret Mitchell's compulsive readers described by Molly Haskell as staying "up all night, reading the book under covers with a flashlight, too young to grasp all its meanings but sensing something utterly fresh about the frank self-interest of a sixteen-year-old girl. . . ." This was the first phase of a happy coincidence that enabled Margie to foresee how she could surpass you in her mother's estimation. She stuck her head into the book because she knew her mother was infatuated with Scarlett O'Hara, having read the novel and seen the movie. If you are an isolated captive, you tend not to know anything about the mind of the tyrant who rules over your life, because that person has contempt for subjects who seek to understand and does not like to be studied. *Gone with the Wind* proved to be a short course on the layout of her mother's mind. The only thing missing from the book was how her mother became Scarlett O'Hara. I happened to learn this one night at the end of our marriage. I think in an unguarded moment she wanted to confess who she was—this should be filed under exit knowledge. She gleaned her vision of happiness looking into the window of a wealthy girlfriend's house—I seem to remember her saying it was raining—she saw her friend and another rich girl lying about, one of them strumming a guitar. The permanent glass between her and her monied friends was constituted by the fact that she lived in the same town in a rent-controlled apartment. She always strove to get into the good graces of rich people, seemingly possessed by the crazy thought that they would eventually share their wealth with her. I can vouch for the fact that the pinnacle of pleasure for her was expensive leisure, although I did not appreciate it at the time. I was dragged to it.

Let's take a stroll down the narrow corridor of Scarlett O'Hara's mind. All the doors are locked except the door to the Bursar's Office, where she lives. Molly Haskell refers to Scarlett as a "predator who marries three men she doesn't love." I can attest to the fact that your mother revealed to me that she did not love me. I was always choked by comparisons. She found a way to nominally cover over this lack, saying "I love you *through* the children." I think the only person she ever loved was her father; and that, in general, she did not love people but situations where the social highlights landed on her. Remember, situations deteriorate; and when they do, she disinvests in them. By reading the book Margie exposed herself to all the evidence that Scarlett was an unloving mother. On the day your mother heard Margie might be hydrocephalic (which she was not), she handed her off to me. (I took her into her room and made a vow that I would stand by her for life.) On that day, your mother together with her mother determined that Margie would always be secondary—a Cinderella—to you. Recall that speaking as a mother, she authored the pronouncement, "It's a good thing for a child to stay in the house alone and do nothing." She once took exception to Margie's statement that "Daddy loves me," and argued with her for an hour that my love was "unresponsible" and "not real" but a form of "game playing." Rhett Butler, who knew Scarlett O'Hara very well, made the following observation, "Ah, Scarlett, how the thought of a dollar does make your eyes sparkle!" Your mother once made an offer to me that was illegal in the State of Vermont, which she never had to answer for in court: you can have more visitation if you pay more child support. She also informed me that I had no right to speak to

Margie during the day because I didn't have a job. She liked to pass off money spent on luxury items for the house—expensive dining-room chairs, fancy drapes, etc.—as "for the girls," when in fact you two had a positive distaste for such things since you knew that each acquisition soon translated into austerity for you. Margie told me she was afraid of her mother's closet because it had "lots of clothes."

What about Scarlett's celebrated *gumption*? Mitchell says of her, "But to her mind there were few, if any, qualities that outweighed gumption." The word first appeared in Scotland in 1719 meaning "shrewdness." Etymologically "gumption" has no connection to "spirit." It has come to mean "have the guts"; in the nineteenth century, it signified "drive" or "initiative." This quality is, unfortunately, related to James Baldwin's favorite line from the movie, "I can't think about that now, I'll go crazy if I do— I'll think about it tomorrow." Gumption is about shutting the mind down, about hardening the original form of your desires, intentions, and utterances by refusing them verbal elaborations. Scarlett has no scruples. I cannot remember any episode in the book where she passes a stone through her conscience. It's like everything out of her mouth is a stipulation—grounds for slapping people. Did your mother ever practice gumption on me? I can honestly say that it was through her that I achieved insight into the meaning of the word. One day I was imploring her to have a conversation in accordance with the divorce document about the welfare of the children. She responded, "You're not going to convince me. When it comes to me, you're talking to a lead wall." In the history I submitted to the court, I found the following incident. She and your stepfather had planned a trip to Florida which entailed that you and I wouldn't see each other for three weeks. Both of you asked for a supplemental visit during the afternoon the week before you left. When I asked her why she would not allow this, she replied, "Because I say so." I then told her that you and Margie were concerned about going so long without seeing me. Her answer to this was, "I believe that, but it doesn't matter."

I read the entirety of *Gone with the Wind* recently and I want to declare it to be an odious book. It is filled with racial vulgarities and I found it hateful to be asked to participate in them. The book twice refers to the "faint niggery smell which crept from the cabin" behind the ruins of Ashley Wilkes' plantation which increased Scarlett's nausea. Scarlett doesn't know that white people have been thought to smell rancid and can stink like full-time liars. When Rhett talks about money lighting up Scarlett's eyes, he asks her, "Are you sure you haven't some Scotch or perhaps Jewish blood as well as Irish?" Mitchell mentions one of the two men who were running Scarlett's lumber mill for her, saying of him, "Anyone could Jew him down on prices." She obviously felt no shame about the dubious trial of Leo Frank, a New York–born Jewish manager of a pencil factory accused of murdering Mary Phagan. He "was sentenced to death amidst courtroom cries of 'Kill the Jew!'" In 1915, the governor commuted his sentence, to great popular outrage. A lynch mob of twenty-five men calling themselves "Knights of Mary Phagan" kidnapped him from prison and murdered him in Marietta, Georgia, near Mary Phagan's house. Mitchell is a Jim Crow person. "At Smith [College], she asked to be removed from a class in which a Negro student was present." She had nothing nice to say about the Freedmen's Bureau and wrote romantically about the Ku Klux Klan, saying at night they dressed up like "ghosts" and "call on" Negroes who are uppity. David Selznick did not want the movie to premiere in Atlanta; but a "battalion of matrons descended like Furies on the mayor's office, which in turn issued a proclamation: 'The movie belongs to all of us' (accent on *us*)." Selznick gave in. Back in 1939, the elite of Atlanta were nostalgic for slave times. At their big cotillion, the Junior League Ball, scheduled the night before the premiere, men wore Confederate grey and women wore hoop skirts. "Atlanta debutantes engaged in a tightly fought contest to see who would wear Scarlett's green gown to the ball." That same night, "the sixty-voice Ebenezer Baptist Church Choir, directed by the Reverend Martin Luther King, Sr., entertained at the whites-only Junior League ball . . . ; choir members, including the ten-year-old Martin Luther King, Jr., were dressed as slaves."

Margaret Mitchell had an unavowed and undiscovered ambition in writing *Gone with the Wind*. She intended to create white folklore that would displace the voice of Uncle Remus which, until her book, had been the most spectacular literary phenomenon ever produced by an Atlantan. There were dozens of businesses named Briar Patch; and restaurants called Uncle Remus's and Brer Rabbit's. "In 1932, Coca-Cola, an Atlanta corporation, distributed more than 3 million cardboard cut-outs and almost 24,000 window display sets, all of them linking the soft drink with Uncle Remus characters." Molly Haskell writes that Mitchell "could hardly explain the way Scarlett took over the book, as if some unconscious compulsion had drawn her demonically onward." That's because she needed a creature to compete with Brer Rabbit. Early in the book, one of the Tarleton sisters, Hetty, says, "'Fast' was the only word for Scarlett." Two years after the book was out, Hervey Cleckley, one of the co-authors of *Three Faces of Eve*, designated Scarlett a "partial psychopath." Mitchell agreed. At a postbellum dance Scarlett feels herself because of her character to be "hunted as a fox." On the next page, she thinks angrily about the other females in the room, "Even though they're poor, they still feel like ladies and I don't. The silly fools don't seem to realize that you can't be a lady without money!" There are important disanalogies between Scarlett's relation to money and Brer Rabbit's relation to life. He is thought by the slaves to be "supple." Scarlett is brittle, much more like Humpty Dumpty. At the end of the book she has a big fall. Because Scarlett is cunning, she does not know that "*Bad means bad*." There is a much more elegant version of this tautology in Chapter 96 of *Moby Dick*: *Accept the first hint of a hitching tiller*. Brer Rabbit lived by this maxim.

Every mention of rabbits in *Gone with the Wind* is either derogatory or about eating them. The most offensive slander is made by Scarlett about her sisters to Mammy, "They haven't any more spirit than a rabbit. . . . At this defiant heresy, Mammy's brow lowered with indignation." Forty pages earlier, Mitchell tries to break the reader out of idiomatic usage by inventing an oxymoron to describe a brood of poor-white children. She combines the words "sullen," a term normally reserved for a slave whose spirit is withdrawn, and "rabbity-looking." Scarlett says of Melanie Wilkes, "How did that little rabbit ever get up spunk enough to stand up to old lady [an opinionated matron] Merriwether?" She describes her second husband, Frank Kennedy, as "so shy! He reminded her of a timid old brown field rabbit."

A returning Confederate soldier asks Scarlett if she has any chewing tobacco; she answers, "Nothing but rabbit tobacco. Pa smokes it in a corn cob." He replies, "I haven't fallen that low yet." Belle Watling, the most notorious madam in Atlanta, built a new bordello for her business, "a large two-story building that made neighboring houses in the district look like shabby rabbit warrens." Late in the book in the middle of a dispute, Rhett says to Scarlett, "Your heart's going like a rabbit's. All too fast for mere fondness I would think, if I were conceited." The suggestion is that Brer Rabbit is not a "fambly man" and devoted to his wife and their "little rabs."

This is what Mitchell meant when she wrote to *The New York Times* reviewer, "And I sweat blood to keep it from being like Uncle Remus." It wasn't simply about dialect; she took a relaxed approach to the way Georgian Blacks talk, readable and phonetic with none of the grammatical stumbling blocks included. She was out to denature the central figure of the slaves' allegory of the Old South so that their vision would collapse for white Southerners. Mitchell was doing something that was anathema to anyone who cared about Black folklore. I think Margie's reading of the book dissolved her internal symbol of the rabbit. After she was done, she began to express some of her mother's conventional social distance toward me. In addition to *Gone with the Wind* providing your sister with a synoptic view of her mother's mind, the other half of the coincidence that seized her was that you began to slide down the social ladder. While staying loyal to you, she found new favor in your mother's eyes and eventually outshined you—she would be admitted to a much more prestigious school than you.

In this section, we have considered three people pursuing happiness—two real, one fictional. It's time for a little excursus on happiness. Happiness should not be pursued; it should be joined. What is the problem that inheres in the pursuit of happiness? In every society that has a class structure, happiness represents what the "better" sort of people understand about the formative steps they can take (self-fortifications) to put themselves in a state of grace with respect to the material good things of life. It's their way of eating a rabbit's foot, of implementing Branch Rickey's (general manager of the Brooklyn Dodgers) axiom: "Luck is the residue of design." Thus from Aristotle's slave culture to our postslavery culture, happiness is defined violently as a certain kind of mastery over life. In the words of Aristotle, happiness (*eudaemonía*) "is the active exercise of the soul's faculties in conformity with excellence or virtue, or if there be several human excellences or virtues, in conformity with the best and most perfect of them. Moreover this activity must occupy a complete lifetime. For one swallow does not make a summer, nor does one day . . . make a man blessed (*makarios*) and happy." So Aristotle says you should strut your stuff for a whole life; and what does he know about time? I became blessed, a macaroon, on the day I met my first blood relative. Two-plus millennia later, we have slightly different lyrics but essentially the same tune from John Rawls' *A Theory of Justice*:

> The main idea is that a person's good is determined by what is for him the most rational long-term plan of life given reasonably favorable circumstances. A man is happy when he is more or less successfully in the way of carrying out this plan. To put it briefly, the goal is the

satisfaction of rational desire . . . ; happiness has two aspects: one is the successful execution of a rational plan (the schedule of activities and aims) which a person strives to realize, the other is his state of mind, his sure confidence supported by good reasons that his success will endure [. . .] happiness is self-contained: that is, it is chosen solely for its own sake.

The problem with these analyses of happiness is that they impose too much conceptual and competitive separation from life. Happiness needs to be plotted; it requires a vantage point where the whole of life can be thought to be projected and deliberated upon. Such a vantage point can be made to exist only to the extent that one *imposes a meaning on life*. If you pursue happiness you have to live with this semantic addition, this lens over life. The Greek word closest to our word "life" is *zoē;* but *bios* as I first learned from Gerald Else, "carries from the beginning the connotation of a *career.*" Skeat derives "career" from the French *carriere* (a race or racecourse) and going full speed on horseback. Aristotle speaking hyperrationally comments in the *Nicomachean Ethics,* "No one allows a slave any measure of happiness, any more than a life (*biou*) of his own." When Socrates describes himself in the *Apology* as someone who refuted lives, the word was *bios*. So what he really refuted were careers. Rawls and Aristotle are talking about a diabolical pact with a future self. Much more common in lives subordinate to a purpose is a syndrome we might call "attachment to means." For the most part the psyche resists being strung out in linear time, for years on end. In any protracted situation your soul will nose around until it establishes its schedule of satisfactions—typically in a denied or misnamed form—and from this position it will silently go about removing the wheels from the plan because it is comfortable where it is.

A remark from Wittgenstein's *Zettel* makes it clear how refractory the pursuit of happiness is: "'Only the intended picture reaches up to reality like a yardstick. Looked at from outside, there it is, lifeless and isolated.' . . . In this way, when we intend, we are surrounded by our intention's *pictures*, and we are inside them. But when we step outside intention, they are mere patches on a canvas, without life and of no interest to us. When we intend, we exist in the space of intention, among the pictures (shadows) of intention, as well as with real things."

It's not that easy to "step outside" the bridle and blinders of an intention once formed. Intentions are often likened to a command given to oneself. However, because the logic of command requires two distinct parties, the similarity of a command to an intention is usually given up on without realizing how far the analogy reaches. If it's your intention, you are pervaded by the imperative; so where's the room for discussion? Once you form an intention to do something, say, in an hour or next Monday, you have bound yourself to it unless you forget it. You are simply not as free to omit the thing in question as you were before you decided to do it. In the interim, you may have grown estranged from the intended act; and yet, when the time comes, you find yourself compelled by the intention anyway. Second thoughts, it seems, have to be a whole lot stronger than the originating thoughts in order to cut through the *gristle* of intention.

Aristotle and Rawls do not lay down as a precondition for happiness that you must love life. This means that neither of them demonstrate to their reader that if you do not love life, you cannot yourself possess life. Aristotle came from a culture whose dominant aesthetic was one of *awe* (supplemented by derision) and distance. This applies equally to *The Oresteia* and the Parthenon. Aristotle, according to Werner Jaeger, was absorbed by Hellenic heroism, which "appeared to him as the expression of one single attitude towards life, an attitude which scales the heights of life only when it overcomes it." Rawls had an attenuated concept of the person. He refused to identify persons with human beings according to biology or psychology. He saw persons as actors inside moral or political controversies deploying their normative abilities to reason, infer, and judge on the basis of their "two moral powers": (1) the capacity for a sense of justice, and (2) the capacity for a conception of the good.

Events in our lives are illuminated for us in essentially two ways or, to extend the metaphor, by two kinds of light. One kind, which we might think of as rational (or artificial) light, is basically projective. By means of definitions, axioms, inferences, prior interpretations, and arrangements, we shine the light on the matter to be understood.—Melville would call this "ghastly" light.— The other, by contrast, is natural light, which we receive rather than project. It comes to us from the event and the people participating in it. Does it light us up? People give off light, and, if we are receptive and benevolently responsive to them, happiness enters us. Wittgenstein has a lot to say about this: "Joy is represented by a countenance bathed in light, by rays streaming from it. Naturally that does not mean that joy and light *resemble* one another; but joy—*it does not matter why*—is associated with light. To be sure, it might be that this association is taught the child when it learns to talk, that it is no more natural than the sound of the words themselves—enough that it exists." Once again there is a consonant passage in the New Testament: "Do not lay up for yourselves treasures on earth, where moth and rust consume and where thieves break in and steal. . . . For where your treasure is, there will be your heart also. The eye is the lamp of the body. So, if your eye is sound, your whole body will be full of light."

An American from the Colombia Support Network visiting the precarious community of San Jose de Apartadó confirmed Jesus's message about what your heart should be attached to. When he and his group arrived there, "Each person we walked past greeted us with a calm wave or a simple 'hola.' There was a strong feeling of trust and respect before we even knew each other's names. . . ." He asked them how they lived despite the unjust practices of their government and the many brutal armed forces just over the hills surrounding their homes and children. "'Easy,' they told us, 'we have each other.' As our conversation progressed, I realized that life with 'first-world conveniences' tends to produce more stress and anxiety than actual happiness. This community, with only rudimentary indoor plumbing, [and] sparse electricity . . . had a much more evident love for life and each other than any group I could think of back in The States. . . . What this community lacks in money and formal education, they more than make up for in warmth, compassion and lust for life."

People are more and more raised in a culture that teaches us not to gaze into one another's eyes and to be unaffected by casual acquaintances' deaths. Big corporations tend not to want us to care for one another. They have found the Occupy Movement a major irritant because people are giving free food to each other, free health care, shelter at night, free books, and carrying signs that read, I CARE FOR YOU. The whole cultural lesson is reversible. (Don't step on dogma!) Stop making insidious distinctions between people based on their education and wealth. Extinguish anger in yourself. Open yourself up to small influences from people; make yourself like nature which excels in the small. Back to Wittgenstein: "Fine shades of behavior.— Why are they important? They have important consequences." If you have lived in the human dark, surrounded by eyes that don't drink you in; the habit of being hugged by many people (what I call living on the hug line) and friendly, discerning eyes could well restore your power to give off light. The biggest thing you can do is fill yourself up with the music of love—sing it, dance it—relate to people through it. It heightens your feeling of life.

VIII

HOW CHILDREN GET CHEATED OUT OF THEIR HUMANITY

Hence Dilthey saw scientific knowledge as involving the dissolution of the connection with life.
—Hans-Georg Gadamer, *Truth and Method*

Is there a problem about how we talk to children? There surely is. My ongoing supermarket studies (aisles, checkout, parking lot) tell me that there is less secure communication between parents and children than ever. The problem threatens to define and unravel our society from top to bottom. If you do not know how to talk with children, then you do not know how to talk well with whatever category comes after children. Remember, meaning something is like going up to someone. By Aristotle's time, the Greeks had already unlearned enough about how to communicate with children for him to conclude that child rearing is an essentially hit-and-miss affair—definitely not an art. Nevertheless, in this era of the sunset of intuition, I would like to take a few steps toward bringing about a Children's Poetics intended to clash with the grave terms of Aristotle's *Poetics*. I will do this by setting out and discussing four quotations from

Joel Chandler Harris, Henry James, and Elizabeth Bowen, and by elaborating on humanitarian abilities that young children have and people past the age of reason have forfeited. It would be very nice to possess a Children's Poetics before the arrival of the complete dark night of science. The first quote comes from Harris's writing in 1907 with a good measure of autobiography in it.

I. Children are persistently misunderstood, misinterpreted, and *driven back on themselves* [stress added] by adults. I get down to their level, think with them and play with them.

Since first reading this a couple of years ago, I have been hanging onto the phrase "driven back on themselves" like the password to a locked-up self. For me it names a well-remembered, fundamental form of childhood pain. My adoptive father used to fly into a rage when I looked at him at the dinner table as if he were a stranger.

The next quotation comes from Henry James' *What Maisie Knew,* describing the effects Maisie has, by virtue of being a child, on the various adults, including her parents, who have assembled around the carcass of a very acrimonious divorce of which she is the hypocritically disputed center—that is, an unloved point of leverage.

II. She has the wonderful importance of shedding a light far beyond the reach of her comprehension, of lending to poorer persons and things, by the mere fact of their being involved with her and by the special scale she creates for them, a precious element of dignity.

115

In thinking this passage through I am inclined to put weight on the Roman origins of the concept of "dignity," of which James was obviously aware. For Romans, *dignitas* was not the bourgeois virtue we tend to think of (pretty much a style of behavior) but rather a matter and measure of the "glory" (*decus*, another derivation from the idea of light) that attached to one because of one's public office. So the light from Maisie creates temporary magistracies on a special scale like the phosphor of sea foam at night. I know a child four or five years younger than Maisie— she's just shy of two—who does what Maisie does. Her name is Amaris and if you stay open to her she will say "Hi!" to you in earnest every few minutes. Tom Roeper has a section on "Hi!" in his *The Prism of Grammar: How Child Language Illuminates Humanism*: "sheer humanity radiates forth when a child first says 'Hi.' But saying 'Hi' is also a significant mental accomplishment, since *hi* refers to no visible thing. . . . The exact social occasion for greeting is hard to pinpoint. *Hello* does not imply we are acquainted with the hearer, but *hi* usually does . . . children are innately endowed with a particular emotion, call it 'greet,' and they attach this emotion or idea to a word that they hear (in English, *hi*)." "Greet" derives from the Anglo-Saxon *grētan* meaning "to approach, visit, and address." Amaris freshens your contact every time she says "Hi!"

The third quotation comes from Elizabeth Bowen's *The House in Paris*. I immediately recognized the truth of it, but for the longest time I really did not understand it.

III. With no banal reassuring grown-ups present, with grown-up intervention taken away, there is no limit to the terror strange children feel of each other, a terror life obscures but never ceases to justify. There is no end to the violations committed by children on children, quietly talking alone.

I definitely remember suffering this kind of terror at the hands of other children; much of it in the form of so-called narcissistic wounding: a remark about my teeth and a reference to the mole on the right side of my mother's chin. Little children speak *au fond,* without the lets and hindrances of adults, and hear to the root. Bowen's point is not about the subjectivity of children. It is about the objectivity of the kind of terror that they feel. As a hurt child, I did not enjoy hurting other children—I hope I did not dish out too many burns. I only began to appreciate the underlying childhood condition that Bowen is referring to by concentrating on the fact that the cure for it is banality ("to banalize" is like a secret verb coiled up in this passage).

The last quotation comes, once again, from *What Maisie Knew.* It could stand as the epigraph for a future Children's Poetics.

IV. For nobody to whom life at large is *easily* interesting do the finer, the shyer, the more anxious small vibrations, fine and shy and anxious with the passion that precedes knowledge, succeed in being negligible.

Imagine a poetics for an audience or an interlocutor not bored or jaded but to whom life at large (I would have liked it if James had italicized that phrase as well) is *easily* interesting. It is perhaps only a small irony that if we turn this sentence inside out, read it contrapositively, it goes from something that illuminates discourse with children to being a rule of thumb for making

Greek tragedies. For anyone able to neglect the finer, shyer, more anxious vibrations, that is someone in whom knowledge trumps passion, to whom life at large is not very interesting. Greek tragedy depends for its distinctive mixture of pity and terror on someone making a big, tragic size, mistake (*hamartia*); and reaches its highest pitch when that mistake involves misrecognition of a "dear one" (*philos*), a blood relative. O Zeus! I've killed my children! She's my mother! Children are masters of individual identity; it is important to get this straight: "That's not my stuffed animal!" "That's not Santa Claus, it's Uncle Jimmy!" Children are not very adept at the abstract similarities that sort things into kinds or relations. When it comes to individuals and differences, they spook adults. Thus Paul Bloom, an academic psychologist, can write of his fourteen-month-old son, "It was uncanny how accurately he used proper names for particular individuals." So children, in addition to lacking stature (seriousness = *spoudaioi*), with their fine, shy, and anxious vibrations are not the stuff of tragedy because it's hard to pull a switcheroo on them. The same goes for body servants. Odysseus, having returned to Ithaca as a beggar, is recognized by his old nurse, Eurycleia, when she spots a scar on his thigh from a hunting accident before he was married. Here, in a different spirit but calling on the same stratum of experience, belongs the adage, "No man is a hero to his valet." And then, of course, there are dogs. Having been gone for twenty years, Odysseus is also recognized—and more directly so because the recognition does not involve "tokens" (*gnōrismata*)—by his dog Argos. I have felt for a long time that the key to identity is laid up in a tagline from Gertrude Stein's *Geographical History of America* (it contains an enticing enjambment of disparate categories): "I am I because my little dog knows me."

A couple of years ago you wrote me a letter in which you described your identification as a young child over a considerable aesthetic distance of a large brown, stuffed bunny that I gave you when we all lived together. Your mother, true to Scarlett O'Hara, absconded with it and deposited it at the Salvation Army. I am so pleased to have your own account in this book that is addressed to you:

> Dear Dad,
>
> Sorry this has taken me so long to write down. I tried to include as many details as I could about *The Velveteen Rabbit* as I could remember. I hope it's ok.
>
> The bunny itself was dark brown—sort of a chocolatey color with a whiteish, greyish all over (like little extra wisps of grey) which heathered or softened the brown. He was sitting upright on his butt and back legs. He had a pale pink silky lining in his ears (which I think were also upright, not floppy). I remember that they had some "stays" or plastic support inside of them to keep them propped up and that the bunny's right ear was broken during the play (and was slightly flopped/bent) when I got him back. I think he had long, stiff, white whiskers. [Uncle Remus would call that a "mustash."] I think I still had this bunny when we were all still together in Hanover. . . . *After* the divorce (I was maybe 7? not older I

don't think), Mom took us to see *The Velveteen Rabbit* at the Ray School. The play was in the pseudo-amphitheater pit in the assembly area. During the play I was sure that I recognized it. The actors were being *very* rough with it. I brought it up to my mother during the play—she brushed me off. Then I brought it up again on the way home (walking through the halls of the school). I think that the first time I brought it up she said something like, "that's not possible" or pretended not to hear or understand me. At some point she definitely declared the "impossibility" of this. Eventually, after repeated questioning by me (and maybe a nudge from Daniel?), she told me that she had given my rabbit to "Listen" (the Salvation Army store); "because I wasn't using it." She still wouldn't acknowledge that this was my rabbit and tried to separate the two ideas.

I protested that she had no right to give my rabbit away and wanted it back. She made me feel badly about insisting on having him back based first on the idea of having given him to the "poor" and then on the fact that "they" were using him for the play. Eventually he was returned to me, with a broken ear. And the actors confirmed that they bought him at "Listen."

Mostly I remember feeling *very* sure that it was my rabbit during the play and going back and forth with my mother about the [im]possibility of this. And, of course, the guilt trip she laid on me about wanting him back, was how I was made to feel greedy. Sorry about this nasty story.

I love you,

Rebec

Before I answer the question contained in the chapter title, I want to make a very speculative addition to the above material, one that, if plausible, may counter the view that young children only perceive differences: they may be able to discern superstructural developments that indicate whether your mother handled you as a boy or a girl. What I am about to relate is a riddle of sorts that was posed for me over and over by the inaugural sphinx in my life, and that still turns up to this day (although I think the signal is getting weaker). From the beginning, I was too flattered by it to get to the bottom of the phenomenon and too embarrassed by how personally complimented I felt to tell anyone about it. This was a riddle that needed an Antigone for its solution, not an Oedipus. At the age of eleven or twelve, I began to notice that I had the strangest effect on little girls ranging in age from, say, eighteen months to five or six years old (just short of the age of reason). Not all little girls but far too many to write it off as a coincidence. Always the same reaction—long doting stares. I admit that being gawked at by these little creatures was quite a thrill; and I returned the attention. Sometimes these little magnetic episodes would lead to some child standing up in her stroller or craning out of her parent's arms in order to keep looking. Fortunately, Lynn witnessed this a sufficient number of times to know that *something* was up and relieved me of the burden of making silly claims for myself.

121

As you know, two years after discovering that I was adopted, I learned of another secret: namely, that before marrying my adoptive father—and unbeknownst to him—my adoptive mother gave birth to an out-of-wedlock daughter whom she named Terry and left at the Salvation Army, where she was claimed by my mother's sister and raised as my cousin. Relinquishing a child is thought often to be the cause of secondary infertility—to which my adoptive mother succumbed. Not long after finding this out, Lynn came across a passage in D. W. Winnicott's *Playing and Reality* whose bearing on me she understood at once and which ultimately became the basis for my speculation here. It concerns a revelatory moment in the treatment of a man who had been making steady progress in therapy for some years (Winnicott was not his first analyst). But the man felt pessimism because something disturbing in him was always escaping analysis. At this particular session, Winnicott gave into certain promptings—about which Winnicott was emphatic that they had nothing to do with homosexuality—and said to the patient: "I am listening to a girl." Between the two of them, they were able to establish that the patient's mother had "held him and dealt with him in all sorts of physical ways" as if he were a girl. They were forced to conclude that the mother had been wanting a girl, "saw a girl baby when she saw him as a baby," and was a long time in coming round to thinking of him as a boy. They further established that the patient's suffering had its source not in the need to release the man in him (I think the concept of an "inner man" is a contradiction in terms), but in the need for the girl to be fully acknowledged together with her "rights over [his] body." I now know the origin of a kind of diffuse feminine impulse in myself. My adoptive mother needing somehow to do her part for the baby girl she "relinquished" (the trade term) wound up casting the same sort of spell over me that was put on Winnicott's patient. This is not the place to go into all the residual signs and symptoms of my early life as a girl. Suffice it to say that for as long as I can remember I have always felt more comfortable in a group of girls than with a pack of males. My identifications with males were never as "internal" as those with females; rather, they are superficial. A photograph of me at age three that used to hang in my parents' bedroom was so girlish that I had to tell my playmates who saw it that it was my *dead sister* (not really that far off). Recently, a letter came to light that my father wrote to the adoption agency at the end of the probationary first year of my adoption in which he describes (completely unapprised of the stakes) my mother's reaction to being caught "pink-handed" at her secret little game: "A woman stopped Olive and said, 'My, my! What a beautiful little girl she is.' Olive was indignant. 'Thank you,' she said, 'but she is very much a HE.' Well, no use blaming that woman. Victor, with his curly blond hair, his soft white skin and his good looks would fool anyone, especially when we have a dress on him [!]. Soon he will get his first haircut."

Winnicott thought of his inclination to call his patient a girl as "madness," his own madness, although obviously something induced in him by the actions of his patient. This predicament of having to put an impossible word into play or else face the stoppered consequences of madness is more common than you might suppose. There is a doctor we both know whose behavior (including aversions and lapses that worked right into her practice of medicine) finally began to make sense to me when one day I declared to myself, "She does not have a mouth," a declaration that was accompanied by a very natural image of her face without a mouth (but not "missing" a mouth). The inertial tendency of almost all her behavior was toward fomenting this conclusion in you. She spoke sparingly in mostly prefabricated packets of words and, where possible, would hum rather than articulate. One was supposed to attend to her eyes, her "good feature," and not her mouth, which had the feel of an abandoned property and was never put into the expressive limelight. She certainly never spent time in the formation of a puckered demeanor saying, "prunes and prisms." And yet she could hover over a plate of food and be rapacious, somehow managing to give you the impression that she ate not with her mouth but her face. I knew her to be haunted ("disgusted" was her word) by memories of her mother, who had a caustic mouth, walking around the house in a brassiere. Since she does not have a mouth, we know of course that she never had any use for her mother's breast. Not examining your patients' mouths closely can limit you as an internist. I have a hole in my gum to this day because of an undiagnosed infection that led to a cyst; I suffered for two weeks thinking I had throat cancer (my favorite song became Chico Buarque's "Morro Dois Irmãos"). It turned out to be post-nasal drip. It was a step toward sanity to recognize that she had negated mouths.

So my speculation about the little maenads I used to pass on the street is this: they were having a full-fledged experience of thinking without being able to say it: "There is a boy who is a girl." They were taken with me because it excited them to see one of their own on the other, freer, side of the fence. Gender strikes me as a concept that has deep roots in perception (and proprioception), much deeper than the public criteria attaching to the use of the words "boy" and "girl," which seem not so much planted in perception as notched into it. Remember I said that the gawking phenomenon seemed to expire around the "age of reason," which, on the hypothesis I am making, would mean that the verbal marks of gender were now in a position of strong precedence over the primordial indicators. That is to say, we now have a child ripe for confusion. I think a young child, if given time, would catch on to the doctor's negation of the mouth. My thesis is that children are extremely sensitive to the normal development of concepts that they are spontaneously acquiring.

Consider what a small part verbal definitions play in the child's acquisition of the concepts it uses in its everyday life—"spontaneous concepts"—and what an enormous part such definitions play in erecting the scaffolding of logic. A child whose thought deployed adult levels of "coherence" and "systematicity," that is, a child with adult susceptibilities to logic, would be one who was cheated out of childhood. As the great Russian psychologist L. S. Vygotsky observed: "A child's everyday concept, such as 'brother,' is saturated with experience. Yet, when he is asked to solve an abstract problem about a brother's brother, as in Piaget's experiments, he becomes confused. . . . Asked to define the concept of 'brother,' the child turns out to be captured by the logic of the actual situations, and cannot approach this concept as an abstract one."

So let us say that children start out as "situationists" (immediate situationists), and that they learn language by playing through, as it were, that is, by doing something in a given situation with a particular piece of language, and that they stay biased toward this form of learning for a long time. (Then comes the "reading trauma.") This accords with what Winnicott averred when he undertook the psychoanalytic treatment of a little girl nicknamed "the Piggle" when she was two years and four months old, continuing until she was five: "It is not possible for a child of this age to get the meaning out of a game unless first of all the game is *played and enjoyed*. As a matter of principle, the analyst always allows the enjoyment to become established before the content of play is used for interpretation" (i.e. before you build anything on it). We seem to have come round again to what Henry James knew, well before professional psychologists descended on children. Writing of Maisie: "She was at the age for which all stories are true and all conceptions are stories. The actual was the absolute, the present alone was vivid." Children, therefore, inside their sphere of operations, are decidedly *not* fantasts (contrary to Sigmund Freud and Lucien Lévy-Bruhl), but much more like hard-headed, fussy, realists. The more so if we agree that the child's world, while limited to the reach of the immediate, nevertheless contains more emotional-perceptual detail per square foot than any stretch of the adult world. Children have to be led out (*educare*) of these originally vivid worlds. Why, then, do so many adults have insuperable difficulties talking to children? Quite simply because they refuse to leave their conning towers (a problem aggravated by status consciousness). When it comes to communicating with children the watchword is "down." This should be taken in the first instance to mean literal, physical (not intellectual) down; eye-level with the child, on one's hands and knees. Only then does one enter the amphitheater of legs, shoes, the underside of tables and shortened horizons where the child lives and plays. Winnicott and Piggle spent the entirety of their time playing with toys on the floor of his office.

There is a juncture which makes us cry if we have to ferry our loved children across it. The very dynamics is best described by Russian developmental psychologists Lev Vygotsky and A. R. Luria who follow the children into self-consciousness about language (a primary source of distortion for Wittgenstein). Vygotsky renders it as the distinction between "spontaneous" concepts and "scientific" concepts; Luria adheres to the same distinction using the terms "mundane" and "academic." Both point to the profound impact of schooling, broadly understood, on the psychology of children; with particular emphasis on the advent of literacy and the development of a more theoretical or conscious attitude toward language. Where before they just *used* words, now children learn that words have correct spellings, grammatical characterizations, definitions, and logical relations. Spontaneous (or mundane) concepts like "girl," "brother," "home," "chair," "pain," "dream," "food," etc., have their inception in experience, in face-to-face encounters, inside actual situations. They grow in their very detailed fashion from the bottom up. Scientific (or academic) concepts such as "peer group," "liberty," "respiration," "acid," "force," etc., start with definitional clarity and move downward toward a more elementary and concrete level. Children are first exposed and become accustomed to systematic reasoning in connection with concepts of this latter sort. Vygotsky further observed that "systematic reasoning, being initially acquired in the sphere of scientific concepts, later transfers its structural organization into spontaneous concepts, remodeling them 'from above.'"

As I understand it, by far the most important part of this top-down remodeling involves getting the child to bring various verbal definitions to bear on its spontaneous concepts and the objects that fall under them so as to open the child up to new groupings. The untutored child thinks in terms of practical ensembles: the Mommy, the Daddy, the children, and the house all go together. But the child who has been initiated into the definition of the word "mother" can be readily induced to put together into one group all and only those things that are mothers. The word "like," which originally has the sense of "having an affinity for or belonging together as a unit," now takes on the new meaning (which enables the odious act of comparison) of "sharing an attribute." The child's thinking is becoming more nimble, flexible, and this is because it more readily takes seriously—is prepared to do something on the basis of—the same word or description applying to different objects. Here we should enter our first demur: it's from Wittgenstein, "The egg-shell of its origin clings to any thinking, shewing one *what* you struggled with in growing up. What views are your circle's testimony: from which ones you have had to break free." By programmatically increasing the child's logical abilities, have we not *ipso facto* opened up a new distance between the child and its world? And who is the trustee of that distance? As the child grows into new abstract ways of connecting items in its experience, who is to say that the prevailing conceptual linkages do not systemically throw portions of its childhood into the dark? In this stitching of experientially grounded concepts into the net of scientific (knowledge-like) concepts, one can almost see the very process Beatrix Potter was glad to have been spared: the rubbing away of originality. Vygotsky has provided an aphorism (a kind of stereoscopic slide) that enables us to consider what a breathtaking development this is: A young child thinks by remembering; an adolescent remembers by thinking. Operating in an environment that has been marked up for logic, the child acquires some interesting new abilities. For example, something that directly bespeaks the factor of distance, the child can now *narrate* its own behavior, implying an ability to maintain a steady face to the outside world. Another enhancement concerns the child's ability to *plan*—and here we should enter a second round of even graver hesitations. The child begins to be able to use the various systematic connections that have been elaborated around it to orient itself and take steps toward objects and goals removed from the immediate environment but whose very existence and nature must be taken on trust, that is, on the individual or collective say-so of third parties. The child has grown colder.

THE RABBIT BETWEEN US CAME FROM SLAVERY

Is it remotely possible that Brer Rabbit swinging from a rope is bearing a deeper and more vicious and prophetic complex than the one Oedipus lugged up to Thebes? I believe so because I agree with Eric Williams's theory of slavery. He wrote in 1944, "Slavery was not born of racism; rather, racism was the consequence of slavery." Wittgenstein espouses the same theory (but we need to make an Albert Murray modification in the quote from him): "A tribe that we want to enslave. The government and the [social] scientists give it out that the people of this tribe have no souls; so they can be used without scruple for any purpose whatever." Wittgenstein believes, according to Stephen Mulhall, "that nothing is more human than the desire to deny the human, to interpret limits as limitations . . . ; Wittgenstein's philosophical practice aims not so much to eradicate this apparently ineradicable hubris but instead to diagnose it and to track down the specific causes and inflections of its endlessly renewed realization in particular cases." James H. Cone, an African American theologian, writes, "The reality of slave existence was brutal; a small assertion of one's humanity might result in death."

David Brion Davis says in *The Problem of Slavery in Western Culture,* "Yet slavery had always been more than an economic institution; in Western culture it had long represented the ultimate limit of dehumanization, of treating and regarding man as a thing. How was one to reconcile the brute fact that slavery was an intrinsic part of the American experience with the New World as uncorrupted nature, as a source of redemption from the burdens of history . . . ?" I am citing experts here—and will continue to—because I don't want you to take my word for any judgment of slavery. All through grammar school, high school, and college, "slavery" was just a word to me; nobody ever taught me about how slaves lived or about the Middle Passage. Slavery is an original sin of America and it is visited upon all future generations. We have lived through the rollback of the first Reconstruction. Upwards of five thousand African Americans have been killed by lynch law. We are living through *The New Jim Crow* (a book every American should read), the rollback of the Civil Rights

Movement. "The United States imprisons a larger percentage of its black population than South Africa did at the height of apartheid." Essential to justice in any form is the implementation of the rule, "Hear the other side" (*Audi alterem partem*). It is a simple fact about justice that the life of the concept shrinks where discussion about its content is blocked or impeded; and hypocrisy on the part of those in power is a fatal impediment. (Ronald Reagan started the War on Drugs when drug use was declining; television lies about the availability of public defenders.) We never hear about the West African belief that the highest form of morality is sharing and generosity. Many don't know the work of Albert Murray: "Again and again the assumption of the surveys is that slavery and oppression have made Negroes *inferior* to other Americans and hence less American. . . . In point of fact, however, slavery and oppression may well have made black people more human and more American while it has made white people less human and less American." Given that the Supreme Court has been whittling away at the Fourth Amendment (search and seizure) and the Eighth Amendment (cruel and unusual punishment), better to sing along with D'Angelo, "Ain't no justice, It's just us."

Orlando Patterson divides slavery into three constituent elements which are very intelligible: (1) First and most distinctive, slavery is always conceived as having originated as a substitute for a usually violent death; not a pardon but a conditional commutation. (2) The slave suffers "natal alienation," the loss of ties of birth in both ascending and descending generations. (3) Slaves are dishonored by the larger society in a generalized way. We need to explore a millennial question with Patterson. "Honor," as Hobbes defines it in *Leviathan,* "consisteth only in the opinion of power." So that to honor someone is to think the value of his or her power high, and to dishonor someone is to rate it low. Patterson thinks of the slave's primal act of submission as a violation of the near-universal belief that "a person's honor is more valuable than his life, and that to prefer life to honor betrays a degraded mind." This near-universal belief does not square with the New Testament. (Patterson knows that.) Paul wrote of Jesus in the Philippians, "He, having the divine nature from the outset, thinking it no usurpation to be called God's equal, emptied himself into the nature of a slave, becoming like to man." Romano Guardini said in *The Humanity of Christ,* "He is never concerned with upholding his own honor." As closely as Patterson comes to how it goes in the world, I find his words in need of modification. Men of honor blink very slowly. Honor is a sarcophagus, a step away from life and toward death. We need to hear about the slaves in the U.S. South: "most slaves did not succumb to the spirit-breaking thrust of plantation discipline. . . . For the most part slaves . . . clung to life tenaciously . . . [and the] strong sense of stewardship in the quarters—of collective responsibility for each other—probably accounts for the low rate of suicide"; much lower than that of the white population both during and after the slave era. John W. Blassingame states in *The Slave Community,* "A communalism born of oppression led to an emphasis on mutual cooperation, joyful camaraderie, respect for elders, and an undisguised zest for life."

Slavery has slipped out of an idiom; it used to be referred to as "the *peculiar* institution"; it is now beginning to go by the far less euphemistic designation "the *perennial* institution." Thanks to the War on Terror and the War on Drugs, a form of totalitarianism is spreading through this country. We are living through enhanced police powers: SWAT teams, riot gear, preventive detention, weapons donated from the Pentagon, the weakening of *habeas corpus* and the Posse Comitatus Act, and the near-automatic reading of the Riot Act whenever dissidents announce their intention to assemble in public. Sheldon Wolin in his recent *Democracy Incorporated* has characterized it as "inverted totalitarianism," which essentially projects power inwards; and aims not to split off one segment of the population from another, but to effect what Wolin would call a complete disaggregation, that is, to fracture or mediate all human ties one by one in society. Marxists have long understood this sort of thing as an internal tendency of capitalism; their word for it was "atomization." As Wolin is careful to note, the "genius" of inverted totalitarianism "lies in wielding total power without appearing to, without establishing concentration camps, or enforcing ideological uniformity, or forcibly suppressing dissident elements so long as they remain ineffectual." The real *point d'appui* of inverted totalitarianism is, however, the *power to depict* and ultimately *to filter* what is happening or being expressed. Individuals are to spend their time in communicational dungeons. Electronic conversation has meant the wholesale loss of facial and intonational nuance.

For us in our private slave society, hardly a week went by without your mother, living in the Big House, promulging (I use this old Walt Whitman verb for the disappointed echo of milk or kindness) some "new rule" designed to further bottle up our imaginative contact with one another. I now believe that the great glory of the Brer Rabbit tales—and of their descendant, the rabbit symbol—is their ability to counteract the dulling effects of living inside an inverted totalitarian regime. In my opinion, the only literary productions that are as contemporary as the Brer Rabbit stories (corporations are looking to *eat* you) are those of Samuel Beckett beginning with *Watt*. In conscience, the Early Socratic Dialogues belong here too. Neither Beckett nor Uncle Remus throw the blanket of fiction over your head. Their stories cycle right into your life in the form of semi-permanent attitudes. I like to think of it as the literature of *porosity*, engaging exercises that enable you to see the holes in the world. With Uncle Remus, it's the holes in situations; with Beckett, the concern is the holes in idioms, rhetoric, and semantics. Had Beckett written animal fables, his hero would have been Brer Worm. Taken at full strength, both of them leave you feeling very well cared for.

I am about to wax theoretical about Brer Rabbit. Let me ask for the grandfathered forgiveness of Uncle Remus (George Terrell, one of the originals, say) for poking around the structure of the animal fable in ways that surely would have annoyed his Socratic instincts:

> Dat de reason I don't like ter tell no tale ter grown folks, speshually ef dey er white folks. Dey'll take it an' put it by de side er some yuther tale what dey got in der min' an' dey'll take on dat slonchidickler grin [slantways oblique] wat allers say, "Go way, nigger man! You dunner what a tale is!" An' I don't—I'll say dat much fer ter keep some un else fum sayin it.

I have always connected Socrates and Uncle Remus in my imagination. When I used to tell my class about Socrates being at home in the suburban deme of Alopece cooking up cross-examinations for prominent Athenians, I used to intone "Way out in Alopece" exactly as I would say "Way up on Chicopin Hill." There are much less contingent connections between them. Both Jesus and Socrates to make themselves intelligible to the uneducated classes of humanity spoke in the wake of Aesop. When Jesus learned that Herod wanted to kill him, he called him "that fox." Jesus resorts to fabular understanding very frequently. The Holy Spirit descends on him like a dove when he is being baptized. "How often would I have gathered your children together as a hen gathers her brood under her wings, and you would not!" There's the brood of vipers, the camel that is stopped by the eye of a needle, the ox that fell in the well, sheep without a shepherd. John saw Jesus coming toward him, and said, "Behold, the Lamb of God, who takes away the sins of the world!" Socrates describes himself in the *Apology*, "It is literally true, even if it sounds rather comical, that God had specially appointed me to this city, as though it were a large thoroughbred horse which because of its great size is inclined to be lazy and needs the stimulation of some stinging gadfly. It seems to me that God has attached me to this city to perform the office of such a gadfly." In the last days of Socrates' life he spends his time, in answer to a dream, versifying Aesop's fables. He is reversing what many believe is "the route by which the fable entered prose, . . . [it] was clearly through the Socratic school . . . This is not at all strange, given the colloquial and popular tone of the Socratic dialogue." Socrates salutes Aesop for the conceptual lucidness of the fable. "I am sure that if Aesop had thought of it, he would have made up a fable about them [pleasure and pain], something like this—God wanted to stop their continual quarreling, and when he found that it was impossible, he fastened their heads together; so wherever one of them appears, the other is sure to follow after. That is exactly what seems to be happening to me. I had a pain in the leg from the fetter, and now I feel the pleasure coming that follows it." The segments of the fable correspond to the natural joints of the concepts. Socrates in Xenophon's *Memorabilia* refers like Uncle Remus to the time they say when animals could talk. I think they're remarking on the era before the urban revolution when people found animals more comprehensible. In the *Phaedrus* Socrates tells the fable of the cicadas, devotees of the Muses who are singing overhead in the trees. If Socrates and Phaedrus win the cicadas' respect, the Muses might send them the gift of needing no sustenance, but of singing and dancing without food or drink until the day of their death. (They won't notice their deaths). One of the earliest Socratics, Antisthenes, says in Xenophon's *Symposium*, "I think, gentlemen, that men's poverty and wealth is to be sought for, not in their estates, but in their souls"—an essentially Socratic view. He learned his hardihood from Socrates, and used to call better-born Athenians snails and wingless locusts.

Both Socrates and Uncle Remus had a talent for something that came to be called *anakrisis*: a technique for provoking or eliciting words from their interlocutors. In Socrates' case, getting them *to say* something; with Remus, getting them to generally *ask* something. In Harris's last book, *Told by Uncle Remus*, Remus is dealing with the son of the original white boy. Uncle

Remus is quite aware that his mother is raising him as a girl and that the little boy is shy and is additionally not talkative because he has been taught that it is impolite to ask questions—when it is, in fact, via questions that a child's conversation proceeds. Uncle Remus tells the little boy, "Honey, you look so much like Brer Rabbit dat I bleeze ter laugh. . . . Yasser, dey ain't no two ways 'bout dat—you look like Brer Rabbit when he trying' fer ter make up his min' whedder to run or no."

Uncle Remus can no more be said to be simply a storyteller than Socrates can be labeled someone who merely reasons. Both do what they do inside conversation; they try to open people up. Sometimes Socrates tells stories and sometimes Uncle Remus disputes. Either way, both fill out their discourse with generous amounts of incidental commentary and a *strong layer of musicality*. This may not be so well appreciated about Socrates, but it is certainly no small part of the Socratic effect as Alcibiades describes it in the *Symposium*: "The only difference between you and Marsyas [the mythical flute player] is that you need no instruments; you do exactly what he does, but with words alone. . . . I swear to you, the moment he starts to speak, I am beside myself: my heart starts leaping in my chest, the tears come streaming down my face. . . . I have heard Pericles and many other great orators, and I have admired their speeches. But nothing like this ever happened to me: they never upset me so deeply that my very own soul started protesting that my life—my life!—was no better than most miserable slaves." Early on in their acquaintance, the little boy failed to show for an appointment to ride out together to a distant part of the plantation to fetch a wagonload of corn. Uncle Remus learned that the boy had been confined to the parlor as a punishment for having wiped his mouth on his coat-sleeve. Seeing that the parlor windows were up—Remus thought of the room as a dungeon—he stood outside and "began to sing about Little Crickety Cricket, who lives in the thicket. Naturally, this song attracted the attention of the little lad, who had exhausted whatever interest there had been in an album and was now beginning to realize that he was a *prisoner*." Socrates' words are meant to stop you in the exercise of false freedom, to get you to see yourself in your "actions," as distributed over cases. Uncle Remus's words, by binding you in one story after another to the character of Brer Rabbit, make for a kind of piece by piece working through of the virtue of suppleness, all with the aim of ridding you of the self-administered portions of your slavery. Both address themselves to the underlying reality of the great expressive object: the self, the soul. Socrates looks fundamentally to increase the coherence of the self. Late in *Told by Uncle Remus,* Harris describes Remus as having been "the first to deplore the system that seemed to take all the individuality out of the little fellow." It might surprise you that one of the supreme values among the slaves was individualism, so they could practice humanism in the slave quarters or out in the woods at the praise house. The Dockerys were baffled when people showed up at the big house to hunt down Charley Patton's distinctive blues style.

We have to deal with some scandalous remarks that June Jordan has made about Brer Rabbit: "With lamentably few exceptions, the Uncle Remus stories center on a pathological hustler, a truly bad rabbit. . . . Premeditated violence, compulsive cruelty, exploitation of children and regular opportunism abound.

Add to these characteristics a fundamental laziness (why can't Brer Rabbit grow his own darn cabbages and carrots, for example?)." She hasn't figured into her critique the love of the slaves for Brer Rabbit. They identify their sensitivity with his, "He got a mighty quick eye, mon, en he tuck notice dat ev'ything mighty still." The joint knowledge of the tales enabled slaves to signal where they were, and avoid the danger of forgetting. When I taught I wanted to personalize my teaching (tear down the formalities), so I acquainted my students with the "strange" (*atopos*) ways of Socrates. When I showed up at an odd time or place, they were primed and ready to go. June Jordan doesn't know that in the Harris tales, *Uncle Remus and His Friends,* Brer Rabbit maintained his own salad garden. She leaves out that he was a terrific singer and quite a musician. He played a panpipe made out of quills. In one story, Brer B'ar hollers to Brer Rabbit, "'You er one er deze yer graveyard rabbits, dat what you is.'" A slave from South Carolina reports seeing Brer Rabbit playing a fiddle on a grave in Red Hill Churchyard and says, "de snow on de grave crack an' rise up, an' de grave open an' I see Simon [Brown] rise up out er dat grave. I see him an' he look jest as natu'al as he done 'fore dey bury him." Lawrence Levine writes that "Brer Rabbit's victories became the victories of the slave. This symbolism in slave tales allowed them to outlive slavery itself." I have an idea where a good bit of that symbolic force derived from. Let me lay it down with Sterling Stuckey that, "slave consciousness was grounded in a continuing awareness of the fundamentals of African faith." Brer Rabbit manifests a striking resemblance to the Yoruba god of individuality, Eshu-Elegba. They both have protuberant eyes and knife-like elements that rise out of their heads. Eshu-Elegba brings to the people *àshe*: "the power-to-make-things-happen, God's own enabling light rendered accessible to men and women." He provides the people with the energy they need to spend on individualism. I love Henry Louis Gates' translation of *àshe* as *logos* because he has supplied an essential connection, inadvertently, between Brer Rabbit and language which I worked on in Chapter V. He is a magnificent interpreter of what other creatures say to him. He's great at hermeneutics. To listen to him is to have a path opened for you. Uncle Remus says, "Brer Rabbit wuz de soopless [supplest] creetur gwine." The word came from the French *soupple* meaning "supple, limber, tender, pliant" out of the Latin *supplicem,* accusative of *supplex* in the old original sense of "bending under," hence submissive. Brer Rabbit taught the slaves to live in Limbo. June Jordan fails to mention that Sufi poet Jalaloddin Rumi versified a straight-ahead Brer Rabbit story into the *Masnavi,* often called the Persian Koran. He frees all the other creatures from the lion who has been oppressing them. In Persian, the tale is called "The Lion, the Hare, and the Hunted Animals." In Uncle Remus, it's named "Brother Rabbit Conquers Brother Lion." Rumi ends his story with advice typical of Brer Rabbit: "Beware! Don't celebrate this fickle world. / O slave to change, don't act as if you're free."

I had an involuntary memory when I was first working on this chapter two years ago. It pertains to the fables and individuality. Six or seven nights in a row, I looked over the side of the bed to view Ernest Shepard's picture on the cover of *Winnie the Pooh*. It shows Winnie standing in the center of a group of his friends—Rabbit, Owl, Piglet, Kanga, and little Roo—holding a large gift-wrapped box. The picture comes from the last chapter of the book, "We Say Good-Bye," about a party thrown for Pooh. I must have identified with Winnie-the-Pooh because of my first name and Mammy-Bammy Big-Money made a Freudian diagnosis of me as a retentive. Night after night I would draw inexplicable warmth from the picture and murmur something to myself about ". . . friends together . . . ." It was a slow-acting madeleine (the pastry that Proust ate and so recovered some of his past). Eventually, I connected the drawing to snapshots from birthday parties when I was in kindergarten and first grade and other little assemblies of my friends from around the neighborhood. After that I came into the recollection that lay behind the Shepard picture. It had restored a sensibility that had been lost to me since childhood. When I was young I experienced my friends as differing naturally one from another as a rabbit differs from a fox or a fox from an owl. When we think of a creature as a rabbit, we think of it as possessing a nature, rabbit nature. The fables do not use individual personalities to unlock animal nature; they use animal nature to *unlock individuality*. In addition to a human nature, however, or as its finest elaboration, each of the children in my neighborhood (and I mean every single one of them) had an utterly unique individual nature that had everything to do with how they played and how they were to be gotten along with. By the time I was seven years old, I had learned Wendyness, Buckyness, Jackyness, and Joness.

As I grew older the attenuations of moral and social pressure eventually ruined this vision of individuality. I came, stupidly, to see individuals as not much more than inflectional variations on a small number of types. I believe performing the Ring

Shout—a very spiritual dance that allows for personal chanting and improvisation—indemnified the slaves against two elaborate stumbling blocks with individualism described by Rumi and Rousseau. Rumi, in the preface to the *Masnavi,* writes:

—Listen to this reed as it is grieving;
it tells the story of our separations.

[. . .]

I was in grief in every gathering;
I joined with those of sad and happy state.
Each person thought he was my bosom friend,
But none sought out my secrets from within me.

[. . .]

There's no concealment of the soul and body,
Yet no one has the power to see the soul.

Rousseau observed in his *Confessions* that people who reveal nothing of their own feelings deprive you of the courage to reveal what you feel, concluding that "it is, in short, pointless to attempt to see into the heart of another while affecting to conceal one's own."

In my forties I became interested in the proposition "No two snowflakes are alike." I traced the thought back to Wilson A. Bentley of Jericho, Vermont. He took microphotographs of snow crystals and also of young girls in his neighborhood. It was Bentley's judgment that "great as is the charm of outline, the internal ornamentation of snow crystals is far more wonderful and varied." Moreover, it was possible, according to Bentley, to read in these exquisite internal figures the history of each snow crystal and the changes it had undergone as it passed through the clouds. "Was ever life history written in more dainty hiero-glyphs?" Bentley went about answering this rhetorical question in the affirmative. "Yes, on the faces of little girls."

X

AUBADE WITH BRER RABBIT

The question "Real or not?" does not always come up, can't always be raised. We *do* raise this question only when, to speak rather roughly, suspicion assails us—in some way or other things may be not what they seem.

—J. L. Austin, *Sense and Sensibilia*

I dunner what would a happen ter little Riley Rab ef ol' Brer Rabbit ain't come along wid a big load er 'spicions. He call de little Rabbit ter de fence. He talk loud an' he say he [don't want Vicky Rabbit livin' in my parents' bag anymo'.]

—Improvised inside the brackets from *Told by Uncle Remus*

Chapter VII of J. L. Austin's *Sense and Sensibilia* must surely be the best sixteen pages ever written about the word "real." In it, Austin explains that "real" "does not have one single, specifiable, always-the-same meaning." On the contrary, as a word it is what Austin calls "*substantive-hungry,*" by which he means that, in order for it to have a definite sense, it needs to be attached to some something: "a real *diamond*," "a real *shooting*," "real *love*." He also calls "real" a trouser-word. If you're looking at two legs performing in trousers, on the basis of the pant-legs you may judge the legs to be real. He goes on to say that it is the negative that wears the trousers, and we understand "only in the light of a specific way in which it might be, or might have been *not* real." Negative showings override positive showings. Austin might agree with a sentence that orphans huddle under from *The Velveteen Rabbit*, "Real isn't how you are made. . . . It's a thing that happens to you." The subtitle of the book—"Or How Toys Become Real"—is a bit of a decoy because its true subject, the psychological feeling of being unreal, could not be so glibly tossed into the nursery. The attached substantive in this case being something internal and not easily circumscribed—that is, the self—does not put us on sure footing with the sense of the term "real." Nonetheless, the book could hardly be more clear that this feeling is not to be mastered by looking inward (which reveals only sawdust). Let me add in the spirit of Austin's analysis, "the body remains . . . the soul's necessary covering," and Wittgenstein's remark, "the human body is the best picture of the human soul." The body can be a source of suspicions about the soul.

Brer Rabbit is still alive. He lives by crossing boundaries, just like the Greek god Hermes. Here we should include the uncanniest boundary of all, the one between inside and outside. When I was eleven, I saw *Song of the South* and Brer Rabbit left my insides altered and disposed me to connect with new people. Like Hermes he is "male, mobile, master of language and roads, of . . . interpretation, communication and its ambiguities.

. . . He is lord of linguistic illusion. . . . He brings the dead back, ambiguously, to the light." He has a good singing voice. I am not here to excuse Disney's atrocious Jim Crow behavior. He picked Atlanta in 1946 to debut the film, which meant that James Baskett [Uncle Remus] and Hattie McDaniel [Aunt Tempy] were "not allowed to stay in the 'whites only' hotel that housed the cast, nor attend premiere functions sponsored by the Junior League of Atlanta." The Oscars in 1947 viciously rejected the nomination of James Baskett for best actor. They did award him an honorary Oscar for his "able and heartwarming characterization of Uncle Remus, friend and story teller to the children of the world." He died four months later at the age of forty-four.

Song of the South is currently under a cultural *damnatio memoriae* even more total than the sheet thrown over Joel Chandler Harris. I am here to defend the movie for how it can improve white kids. The movie opens with a piece of abracadabra about "real." Disney or no—it's hard to imagine a more effective sequence for calling children out of a very common sort of funk that their parents will have worked hard to keep them in. The action (post–Civil War) begins with Johnny (Bobby Driscoll) riding and talking in an open carriage with his parents (his mother looks like mine) and Aunt Tempy on their way for a visit to his grandmother's plantation where Uncle Remus now resides. The parents are dissembling nonstop about the real circumstances behind their visit (i.e. marital difficulties), which Johnny clearly senses but gets nowhere attempting to question them. The atmosphere is palpably false and uncomfortable. Johnny is getting the hugger-mugger treatment, until Aunt Tempy intervenes about the sound of frogs and Uncle Remus telling tales with no tails. Aunt Tempy slips into our conscious-ness an Austinian preview of the central mystery that the chil-dren in the audience will be undergoing. We are going to be shown "holy things" and something is bound to happen in the soul. Johnny, freshly skeptical from being lied to, asks: "Aunt Tempy?"—"What is it, child?"—"Is Uncle Remus real?"—"Real? Of course he's real! You just wait till you hear him tell a tale about Brer Rabbit, *then you know he's real.*"

A couple of movie-minutes later, we are with Johnny crying hard on the veranda and calling out to his father not to abandon him. The children watching are inside the movie by this time; they have been initiated into the mystery. I took the underlying substantive, often without knowing it, to be *love*. Uncle Remus has a more loving voice and loving look than Johnny's father. Remembering the beginning of change in your personality is often well-nigh impossible because the various elements that combine for change fall into place one by one. Nevertheless, with regard to a certain complex disposition that has never left me, I would have to say that *Song of the South* feels like the origin story. I cry every time I see it. Thanks to the exposure to Uncle Remus, I began for the first time to understand the suppressed quantity in my life—a certain kind of emotional sustenance that was "lost" to me after rejoining my parents. There is a moment in the movie of surpassing seriousness, a moment that could well stand as the emblem of everything I am trying to describe here. It comes at the end of the first animated Brer Rabbit story when the face of Uncle Remus, who has been narrating it all along, breaks through like the moon in the night sky. His expression, even though Brer Rabbit is now safe at home, is one of the utmost concern. Before the lap-dissolve is complete, he speaks the words, "And just like I told him [Brer Rabbit], you can't run away from trouble." I had already identified with Johnny and Brer Rabbit. Given the ominous quality of the scene where Uncle Remus passes for the moon, I feel certain that it was the origin of my lifelong sense that the voice of the moon and the voices of the interpreters of nighttime generally are Black, male, and quite lovely. To begin with, the film supplied me with an object (my parents were paltering with me) that fit the form of my anxieties and melancholy which had previously been objectless for me. The movie switched me from *passive to active*. I now had a direction to move in. It was the sound of life: listen to it, learn to make it.

I latched onto Uncle Remus; I made him my guardian angel. I purchased the 45 RPM records of all the songs and tales in the movie, and every day after school I sat in the sunroom of the house listening to Uncle Remus's beautiful voice and looking at his smiling picture. I believe that I was transferred in my sleep from the orphanage to my adoptive parents' house in Indiana and from there to my grandfather's care who took me on a train to Buffalo and from my grandmother's house six months later to my parents' apartment in Buffalo. I woke up in totally new environments. Since I learned that I was adopted, I wake up with anxious memory lapses in the morning and have difficulty breathing deeply. I discovered that if I read the dialect Uncle Remus in bed, he sets me at my ease. I expect that a similar thing happened to Joel Chandler Harris when he sat in the chimney corner of George Terrell's cabin. You'll recall John Goldthwaite made a comparable discovery about Beatrix Potter, why she started illustrating tales where she did. The story is from *Uncle Remus: His Songs and Sayings*, and its first lines are his greeting. Never had she been recognized as Uncle Remus did the little boy, who arrived with a huge slice of pie he spirited while his mother is off with company. Beatrix and I both spent imaginary time with Uncle Remus, in keeping with the fess point of the dream that Joel Chandler Harris never surrendered, a childhood in an African American world. Beatrix broke out of her family by raking in a lot of money and becoming Aunt Remus for children in the nursery. Uncle Remus healed me; after five or six days with him, I got over my phobia about swallowing [lies]. I used to require a glass of water nearby when I would chew solids (including candy bars).

A critic from San Diego obviously meaning to defend the film upon its re-release in 1986 (I took you and Margie to see it), wrote about enjoying it with "an audience made up largely of happy, responding kids," saying it was like "returning to childhood's innocent treasures." Especially if I was alone in the house, putting on the records, I would fall to dreaming over the picture of Brer Rabbit on the album cover like a portrait of a saint on a devotional card. I internalized Brer Rabbit—became a discipline problem at school and at home—in order to be more intimate with Uncle Remus. For me, and I imagine countless similarly wounded white children, what happened in the theater was more on the order of demonstration than a fantasy, more like being initiated into an ancient mystery cult. My conjecture is that children, particularly those with undernourished selves, can hear into the adult capacity for love. On the basis of such soundings (as they say in the spy world) they can be turned; that is, they come into possession of judgments deeply at odds with their culture.

Shortly after the movie another thing happened to reinforce my new image of life. It was the Doo-Wop era. I used to hear Black kids singing wonderful versions of popular songs ("Silhouettes," "Little Star," "Book of Love," etc.) walking up from Lafayette High School over to the East Side. Doo-Wop with its seemingly endless trove of beautiful songs set at night, eventually my favorite song was "I Only Have Eyes For You" by the Flamingos; before that, I loved "Searchin'" by the Coasters. My favorite line in the latter was, "Gonna find ya." I still play it on the piano. From my neighborhood in Buffalo, the moon at its most splendid seemed to hang like a proprietary object over the East Side where the Black community lived. So my sentiments in this direction "jes grew"—to quote my fellow Buffalonian, Ishmael Reed. When I got old enough I used to spend my weekends at the Pine Grill and Shalimar. One summer day I drove around with Jon Hendricks in my little red sportscar. I dropped him at the Royal Arms in the evening; I parked and went in; the last time I saw him he was singing Tom Jobim's "Corcovado" beautifully.

I moved to northern New England in 1971, and the moon and the night sky got sterilized. Then about seven years ago, I encountered two images almost back-to-back: one that completely elated me, and a second that I found moving to the point of tears. The joint effect of the two was to unblock everything and restore me to warm communications with the nighttime. The first reads like a haiku from Ishmael Reed, "Cab Calloway standing in for the moon." The second is a description from John Szwed's book on Sun Ra, *Space Is the Place*. Szwed writes the

African American "protective societies gave annual balls which were elaborate affairs, displays of elegance and dignity, where foundry workers could move in the same circles as the small number of lawyers and doctors. . . . Manual laborers by day could assume positions of great respect at night. Each ball was thematically keyed to a current hit song. . . . The Knights of Pythias once introduced their members to the music of 'Stairway to the Stars,' each of them descending from the ceiling, stars sprinkled through their hair."

The movie obviously lowered my social inhibitions which I had picked up from my mother, who was hyper-English and had a real dread of poverty. As a result, I became closer to my immigrant, adoptive grandmother who saved my life. When my parents sent me to her house for an extended stay (which they denied, contrary to all the tender evidence she gave), I was a colicky baby. She fed me squab soup and goat's milk, and I lived a lot of my waking hours in her arms or on her lap. When my parents came for me six months later, I was invested with broken English and my grandmother's sounds, basically the phonemes, rhythm, and melody of Italian. Upon arriving at my parents' apartment, my father made a recording of me expressing an urgent communication in flibbertigibbet. Eventually I became a mute aspirant toward my grandmother. The principal form of this was my secret infatuation with her blue parakeet, Petey. I loved how she permitted him to land on the same spot on the frame of the dining-room mirror and let him peck at it and smudge his image. He was allowed to fly around the house and was often perched on her shoulder. I used to sing, "Mr. Bluebird on her shoulder. It's the truth, it's actual. Everything is satisfactual."

Another form of aphasic pining for my grandmother set me up as an early version of the title character from the movie *Man Facing Southeast*—Rances, a leftist interned at a Buenos Aires psychiatric hospital who has the disarming habit of standing in the courtyard and communing with the sky in the direction of southeast. The movie leaves unstated that he is looking toward the point over the water where hundreds of the disappeared, alive and drugged, were thrown from planes into the ocean during the Dirty War. I became the "Boy Facing Northwest," inasmuch as I regularly took to lying on my back in bed, looking out in the direction of my grandmother's house over the tops of a row of poplar trees outside my window. It felt miraculous to me; the leaves always seemed to be shimmering like sunlight on the water.

Having reseen *Song of the South* in 1986, the Disney animators must have been saddled with the Charles-Bonnet syndrome—they are hallucinations of a cartoon-like character. That summer Lynn and I were driving you girls to Montezuma, Georgia, to meet Bernice for the first time. When I hit the two-lane highway on the way to Macon County I felt I was in the cartoony atmosphere when Uncle Remus went for a walk on the big road. Perhaps most embarrassing was the thrill I got from the little sulfur butterflies that arced around the car all the way up the road to Montezuma. I began to think of Uncle Remus singing "Zip-A-Dee-Doo-Dah," with butterflies (some yellow) swooping around him. When I told Bernice how pretty I thought these yellow butterflies were (actually they were plain and pale, hardly a cut above a moth), she gave me a kind of slantways, oblique look that suggested there was something white and northern about this predilection. It was not long before the affection these little flying creatures set off in me began to alight on Bernice, and soon she was using them to send the same feelings back to me. They became for us a private fleet that pulled our names through the air. Lynn and I made approximately ten trips down there over the next seven years. We began to feel that Bernice's trailer was home to us. She would announce our coming in the local newspaper. My father pulled the shades down in the house when I became divorced and made every effort to conceal Lynn from the family. The last time I saw Bernice, it was the year 2000 and she was dying of kidney cancer in a Macon hospital; we looked each other in the eye and said we'd see each other on the other side.

As I finished out my college teaching career, I unconsciously obeyed the rule that Victor Hugo enunciated in *Les Miserables,* "Everybody who has had a mysterious childhood is always ready for certain renunciations." I abandoned my dissertation because I had good reason to believe that my theory behind *The Republic* (The *Techne* Theory) had been plagiarized. I turned down students who offered to protest my punishing dismissal, and one whose name was Lyman who proposed going on the radio to editorialize about what a loss I would be to the college. Inside institutions I always felt my presence was illegitimate: I looked for unconditional love and came to repudiate the explicit procedures for promotion. Twenty years later when I learned I was adopted, I sent forty cartons of books to a friend in Woodstock, Vermont, who ran a used bookstore. I have finally come to regret all these things.

You, Rebecca, may not have heard of this. But I once concluded a course in the history of moral philosophy by disgustedly breaking off my final lecture on Immanuel Kant—telling the students that they had enough deathly language from white men and that we would do well to give the last word on the subject to a Black man; and then I proceeded to play Stevie Wonder's new double album, *Songs in the Key of Life.* From the start, I always inclined toward an old-fashioned understanding of the philosopher's mission; that is, to defend reality against the onslaught of appearances. But true to Austin's admonitions about "real," I took the substantive that philosophy was hungry for—often without knowing it—to be "love" and the crucial issue to be appearances that either distorted or sealed up its presence.

XI

THE RABBIT DANCES

Also the classical theory of art, which bases all art on the idea of mimesis, imitation, has obviously started from the play which, in the form of dancing, is the representation of the divine. But the concept of imitation can only describe the play of art if one retains the element of knowledge contained in imitation.

—Hans-Georg Gadamer, *Truth and Method*

Make a bow ter de Buzzard en
den ter de Crow,
Takes a limber-toe gemmun fer
ter jump Jim Crow.

I have a fantasy that Jesus Christ comes back to Earth and is dis-appointed about how much murder has taken place over these last many generations. He would be making a judgment that echoes what he said in the Lost Gospel, Q, reconstructed by Burton Mack. "We played the pipes for you and you did not dance." "We sang a dirge and you did not wail." He would find that we were much too involved in our possessions and would agree with Wittgenstein that "Hate between men comes from cutting ourselves off from each other." I think he would proceed directly to Rio de Janeiro and climb Corcovado to deliver another miraculous Sermon on the Mount. When he reached the 130-foot statue of himself—the Cristo Redentor, arms wide open, looking down at the Bay of Guanabara—he would make it dance and fill the air with his own music. The song might be called "The Samba de Concreto."

I am old enough to be a cicada. In Socrates' fable about the cicadas, he says that they were men of age before the Muses came to Earth. If I hear danceable music, I feel a boost in my energy level. I have tailored the Plato quote to suit me: "When the Muses came into the world [especially Terpsichorē], and music made its appearance, some of the people were so thrilled with pleasure that they went on [dancing] and forgot to eat [and take their medicine] until they actually died without noticing it." Once I was dancing to "One Note Samba" with the baby,

Amaris, in my arms on the sidewalk in front of Kismet, a restaurant in Montpelier, and when it was over she told me she loved me. Another time Lynn and I were dancing to Eumir Deodato's version of "The Girl from Ipanema" in the parking lot of Angkor Wat, a restaurant in Woodstock, Vermont. Four older people came out and started to dance. These are the kind of pretty things done for no specific reason, little gracious exchanges which, as James Davidson writes in *The Greeks and Greek Love,* "reveal the *psyche*, the personality, because gracious exchanges actually *produce* the personality by allowing it an occasion to perform, to exercise its discretion and space and time to grow. . . . People are people only when they engage with you."

Music is not fiction. The emotions that music produces in you are real. Wittgenstein concurs, "Feelings accompany our apprehension of a piece of music in the way they accompany the events of our life." A rhythm which you have matched creates spontaneity and makes you no longer at the complete mercy of external forces; people singing and dancing obtain relief from oppression. James H. Cone writes, "Blacks were able, through song, to transcend the enslavement of the present and to live as if the future had already come." A Ghanaian drummer, Ibrahim Abdulai, noted, "Music is something which does not conceal things about us, and so it adds to us." Hailing from New Orleans, Wynton Marsalis trumpets the same virtue, "Music makes the internal external. What's in you comes out. . . . Because once the band begins to play, they know that for the next hour and fifteen minutes, everyone . . . will be united in the purest possible expression of community, having made the choice to become 'us' instead of 'me.'"

The seventeenth-century French philosopher, René Descartes, ruined the road from the inner to the outer. He was an extreme dualist, dividing the universe into material substance (*res extensa*) and thinking substance (*res cogitans*). He thought emotions were confined to thinking substance—invisible—and only knowable by introspection. He introduced causation into the vision of the soul and thereby wrecked the heart which can see quicker than the eye. The pineal gland was thought by him to mediate between the soul and the body. He objected to Aristotle's notion, which carried over to Augustine and Aquinas, that emotions were intentional and expressive. Descartes looked at mathematics as a model for the human mind: "those long chains composed of very simple and easy reasonings, which geometers customarily use to arrive at their most difficult demonstrations, gave me occasion to suppose that all the things which fall within the scope of human knowledge are interconnected in the same way." One of the foundations of his thought, which he could not doubt, was "I think, therefore I am" (*Cogito, ergo sum*). He believed he could live without a body. (What would he be doing for other human beings?) He condemned us to have to reason about other minds on the similarity of our behavior. He flattened out the picture of humanity. Twice he speculates in his central work, *The Meditations,* that human figures could be automatons: (1) "I look out the window and see men crossing the square. . . . Yet do I see any more than hats and coats which could conceal automatons?" (2) "I might consider the body of a man as a kind of machine equipped with and made up of bones, nerves, muscles, veins, blood and skin in such a way that, even if there were no mind in it, it would still perform all the same movements" as if it had a mind. Descartes believed that higher animals were automatons, and, absurdly enough, that they could not feel pain. Joan Dayan argues in *Haiti, History, and the Gods* that Descartes taught the French people to live with slavery. She refers to his *Discourse on Method* and *The Meditations* as the "nasty belch" which gave birth to Louis XIV's edict called the *Black Code* (which has never been translated into English). The Enlightenment took a Cartesian step back from the people. Because of the disanalogy in what French and African people willed, "the slave is recognized as having a will only insofar as it is perverted." Wittgenstein in the mid-twentieth century formulated the Private Language Argument to go after Descartes' central mistake: "Nor can anyone know what he means by the word himself [through introspection]; for to know the meaning of a word is to know how to use it rightly; and where there can be no check on how a man uses a word there is no room to talk of 'right' or 'wrong' use."

I have been looking for a logical mechanism to spring humanitarian love between people. My earlier points might have implied it. I found it folded up in my replacement for Descartes' *Cogito, ergo sum*. It's thanks to a Senegalese poet, Léopold Sédar Senghor, obviously outdoing and satirizing Descartes: "I feel the other, I dance the other, therefore I am." He starts off weak with an indeterminate idea about the other. But then he faces his dance partner; and in putting themselves on reciprocal rhythmic display, they enhance each other. It's comparable to being held by your mother and picking up her feeling, her breathing, and her heartbeat. A hug will accomplish some of this. So might a good conversation. We bring one another into being.

I have seen several times Danilo Caymmi and his father, Dorival Caymmi, at a music session at Tom Jobim's house, on a DVD entitled *A Casa Do Tom*. They were standing on opposite sides at the end of Tom's grand piano. I love them both. Danilo played the flute intro to a song Dorival composed, "Maracangalha," and began to sing it. Dorival joined him on the second verse. They smiled and looked warmly at each other the whole time; all were Dorival's compositions. There was not a trace of Oedipal conflict. Danilo took his own part in his father's creativity. I was never in a position to enjoy this kind of concordance with my father.

All this goes to show what James H. Cone ascribes to Martin Luther King, Jr.: "Human beings are made for each other and no people can realize their full humanity except as they participate in its realization for others."

NOTES

CHAPTER I. PSYCHIC BOLT-HOLES

PAGE 1 • "We want to say . . . the thing we mean"—Ludwig Wittgenstein, *Philosophical Investigations* (New York: Macmillan, 1953), §455.

PAGE 5 • "a rough stake and a shapeless piece of wood"—Jeffrey M. Hurwit, *The Athenian Acropolis: History, Mythology, and Archaeology from the Neolithic Era to the Present* (Cambridge: Cambridge University Press, 1999), p. 20, p. 279.

"*xoana* were often thought to fall from heaven"—David Freedberg, *The Power of Images: Studies in the History and Theory of Response* (Chicago: University of Chicago Press, 1989), pp. 34–6.

"Pausanias described such statues"—Jean-Pierre Vernant, *Mortals and Immortals: Collected Essays* (Froma I. Zeitlin ed.) (Princeton, NJ: Princeton University Press, 1991), p. 154.

PAGE 6 • "To the victor, the potatoes"—Joaquim Machado de Assis, *Quincas Borba* (Gregory Rabassa trans.) (Oxford: Oxford University Press, 1998), p. 13, p. 27, p. 266.

PAGE 10 • "One night in June . . . that June night"—Gaspare Giudice, *Pirandello: A Biography* (Alastair Hamilton trans.) (London: Oxford University Press, 1975), pp. 3–4.

PAGE 17 • "the reforestation of Vermont"—Charles W. Johnson, *The Nature of Vermont: Introduction and Guide to a New England Environment* (Hanover, NH: University Press of New England, 1998), pp. 117–19.

CHAPTER II. VISITATION

PAGE 24 • "Ah, your favorites . . . a heap of dead rabbits"—Emily Brontë, *Wuthering Heights* (New York: Alfred A. Knopf, 1991), p. 10.

PAGE 31 • "And magic always rests on the idea . . . of language" —Ludwig Wittgenstein, *Remarks on Frazer's* Golden Bough (Rush Rhees ed. and A. C. Miles trans.) (Doncaster: Brynmill Press, 1979), p. 4.

"a whole mythology . . . our language"—Wittgenstein, *Remarks on Frazer's* Golden Bough, p. 10.

PAGE 32 • "Muhammad is the chamber and Ali is the doorway"—Jean Chevalier and Alain Gheerbrant, *The Penguin Dictionary of Symbols* (John Buchanan-Brown trans.) (New York: Penguin Books, 1996), p. 473.

PAGE 33 • "after tree shrews and flying lemurs"—Susan E. Davis and Margo DeMello, *Stories Rabbits Tell* (New York: Lantern Books, 2003), p. 8.

PAGES 35–6 • "psychoanalytically informed", "preference for privacy"— Joseph Goldstein, Anna Freud, and Albert J. Solnit, *Beyond the Best Interests of the Child*, NEW EDN (New York: Free Press, 1979[1973]), p. 115, p. 7.

PAGE 36 • "a Denver group of pediatricians"—Ian Hacking, *Rewriting the Soul: Multiple Personality and the Sciences of Memory* (Princeton, NJ: Princeton University Press, 1995), p. 60.

"the noncustodial parent . . . visit the child"—Goldstein, Freud, and Solnit, *Beyond the Best Interests of the Child*, pp. 37–8.

"decided to err on the side of non-intrusiveness"—Joseph Goldstein, Anna Freud, and Albert J. Solnit, *Before the Best Interests of the Child* (New York: Free Press, 1973), pp. 136–7.

"the sacrosanct word"—Goldstein, Freud, and Solnit, *Beyond the Best Interests of the Child*, 117ff.

"finding the empty and friendless house"—Grace Metalious, *Peyton Place* and *Return to Peyton Place* (New York: Random House, 1999), p. 12.

PAGE 37 • "comparison is like the hidden worm . . . out of love" —Søren Kierkegaard, *Works of Love* (Howard and Edna Hong trans) (New York: Harper Perennial, 2009), p. 181.

"To arrive at a trustworthy opinion . . . clinicians"—Goldstein, Freud, and Solnit, *Before the Best Interests of the Child*, p. 43.

PAGE 38 • "infantile seduction"—Nicholas T. Rand and Maria Torok, *Questions for Freud: The Secret History of Psychoanalysis* (Cambridge, MA: Harvard University Press, 1997), p. 37.

"there is no societal consensus . . . for all children"—Goldstein, Freud, and Solnit, *Before the Best Interests of the Child*, p. 133.

"Can your mother's depraved remark . . ."—Victor Menza, Unpublished Work on the Court Case (April 1983), p. 65.

PAGE 39 • "least detrimental alternative"—Goldstein, Freud, and Solnit, *Before the Best Interests of the Child*, p. 21.

"the devoutly skeptical Freud . . . hold out"—Erik Erickson, *Young Man Luther: A Study in Psychoanalysis and History* (New York: W.W. Norton, 1993), p. 253.

"Love is not . . . for others"—Kierkegaard, *Works of Love*, p. 211.

"a major thrust of contemporary marketing . . . against the parent"—Juliet B. Schor, *Born to Buy: The Commercialized Child and the New Consumer Culture* (New York: Scribner, 2004), pp. 160–2, p. 16, p. 173.

PAGE 40 • "People with higher financial aspirations"—Schor, *Born to Buy*, p. 174.

"children have no psychological conception . . . their development" —Goldstein, Freud, and Solnit, *Beyond the Best Interests of the Child*, p. 12, p. 23, p. 119.

CHAPTER III. I NEVER SAW HARVEY

PAGE 41 • "Quite sure . . . just then"—Mary Chase, *Harvey: A Comedy in Three Acts* (New York: Dramatists Play Service, 1971), p. 54. Originally published as *The White Rabbit* in 1943.

PAGE 42 • "Old Celtic mythology . . . crackpots"—Henry Koster (director), *Harvey* (Universal International Pictures, 1950). All subsequent quotations from *Harvey* are from the film version unless otherwise noted.

PAGE 43 • "Harvey and I . . . moments of talk"—Chase, *Harvey*, p. 54.

PAGE 44 • "slurs, stumblings . . . triple entendres"—Bruce Fink, *Fundamentals of Psychoanalytic Technique: A Lacanian Approach for Practitioners* (New York: W.W. Norton, 2007), p. 6.

PAGE 48 • "He has made one movie, *Ten*"—Abbas Kiarostami (director), *10 on Ten* (Zeitgeist Films, 2004).

CHAPTER IV. WHAT IS A SYMBOL

PAGE 50 • "The word symbol is a term . . . possible"—Northrop Frye, "The Symbol As a Medium of Exchange" in *Symbols in Life and Art: The Royal Society of Canada Symposium in Memory of George Whalley* (James A. Leith ed.) (Montreal: McGill-Queen's University Press, 1987), p. 3.

"with forks and hope"—Lewis Carroll, *The Hunting of the Snark: An Agony in Eight Fits* (London: Chatto and Windus, 1941), p. 24.

"an old idea . . . over its history"—J. L. Austin, *Philosophical Papers*, 3RD EDN (J. O. Urmson and G. J. Warnock eds) (Oxford: Oxford University Press, 1981), p. 201.

PAGE 52 • "Among the Ndembu of Zambia . . ."—Dan Sperber, *Rethinking Symbolism* (Alice L. Morton trans.) (Cambridge: Cambridge University Press, 1974), p. 29.

"every symbol must in due course . . . needs doing"—Robert Musil, *The Man Without Qualities* (Sophie Wilkins and Burton Pike trans) (New York: Alfred A. Knopf, 1995), p. 637.

PAGES 53–4 • "living momentary revelation", "pregnant moment", "remain inexpressible"—Angus Fletcher, *Allegory: The Theory of a Symbolic Mode* (Ithaca, NY: Cornell University Press, 1964), p. 13, p. 15,p. 17n30.

PAGE 54 • "symbolism is a very profound function of the mind" —Johan Huizinga, *The Waning of the Middle Ages*; as cited in Fletcher, *Allegory*, p. 17n31.

"No symbol where none intended"—Samuel Beckett, *Watt* (London: John Calder, 1976), p. 255.

PAGE 57 • "the buying of Hill Top Farm . . . never completely faded" —Margaret Lane, *The Tale of Beatrix Potter: A Biography* (New York: Penguin Books, 1986), pp. 87–8.

CHAPTER V. DOWN THE PHILOSOPHICAL RABBIT-HOLE OR "GAVAGAI!"

PAGE 60 • "I look at an animal . . . he sees"—Wittgenstein, *Philosophical Investigations*, Part II, p. *xi*.

"The utterances first . . . further cases"—Willard Van Orman Quine, *Word and Object* (Cambridge, MA: MIT Press, 1960), p. 29.

PAGE 61 • "the forces he sees . . ."—Quine, *Word and Object*, p. 28, p. 29, p. 45, p. 39.

PAGE 63 • "a very pleasant and vivacious manner"—Ian G. Kennedy, *Titian, Circa 1490–1576* (Cologne: Taschen, 2006), endorsement on the cover; originally quoted in Giorgio Vasari, *Lives of the Artists* (1550).

"life, and the life was the light of men"—John 1:5.

"continual solitude that envelops Jesus"—Romano Guardini, *The Humanity of Christ: Contributions to a Psychology of Jesus* (Ronald Walls trans.) (New York: Random House, 1964), p. 48.

PAGE 64 • "There, after days and days . . . encounter rabbits"—Italo Calvino, *Marcovaldo, or The Seasons in the City* (William Weaver trans.) (San Diego, CA: Harcourt Brace Jovanovich, 1983), p. 52.

"The idea of life . . . of life"—Michael Thompson, *Life and Action: Elementary Structures of Practice and Practical Thought* (Cambridge, MA: Harvard University Press, 2008), p. 25, p. 27.

PAGE 65 • "Wittgenstein accepted the very same challenge"—Wittgenstein, *Philosophical Investigations*, Part II, p. *xi*.

"We feel that even if *all possible* . . . answer"—Wittgenstein, *Tractatus Logico-Philosophicus*, 6.52.

"Wittgenstein's later work is very *oral*"—Stephen Mulhall, *Philosophical Myths of the Fall* (Princeton, NJ: Princeton University Press, 2005), pp. 119, 95, 122–3.

PAGE 66 • "he discusses the 'rabbit' exclamation"—Ludwig Wittgenstein, *Last Writings on the Philosophy of Psychology*, VOL. II (C. G. Luckhardt and M. A. E. Aue trans) (Chicago: University of Chicago Press, 1982), p. 16.

"If someone sees a smile . . . who understands it?"—Wittgenstein, *Philosophical Investigations*, Part II, p. *xi*.

PAGE 67 • "If one thought . . . what people feel"—Elizabeth Bowen, *The Death of the Heart* (New York: Anchor Books, 2000), pp. 403–04.

"Verbal language . . . cadences", "For can anything be . . . of it" —Ludwig Wittgenstein, *Remarks on the Philosophy of Psychology*, VOL. I (G. H. von Wright and Heikki Nyman eds, C. G. Luckhardt and M. A. E. Aue trans) (Chicago: University of Chicago Press, 1980), §888, §1090.

"talks about the exclamation point"—R. W. Burchfield (ed.), *The New Fowler's Modern English Usage,* 3RD EDN (Oxford: Clarendon Press, 1996), p. 273.

CHAPTER VI. THE RABBIT EVANGELS

PAGE 69 • "*Uncle Remus* was her reference point . . . humans overlap" —Linda Lear, *Beatrix Potter: A Life in Nature* (New York: St. Martin's Griffin, 2007), p. 131.

"Rudyard Kipling was a great fan of Harris"—Walter M. Brasch, *Brer Rabbit, Uncle Remus, and the "Cornfield Journalist": The Tale of Joel Chandler Harris* (Macon, GA: Mercer University Press, 2000), p. 82.

"The latter supports Alice Walker's accusation . . ."—Alice Walker, "Uncle Remus, No Friend of Mine," *Southern Exposure* 9 (Summer 1981): 31.

"In the words of Augusta Baker . . ."—Julius Lester, *Uncle Remus: The Complete Tales* (New York: Dial, 1999), p. *viii.*

PAGE 70 • "garbled forms of high diction mark Harris's texts"—Page duBois, *Slaves and Other Objects* (Chicago: University of Chicago Press, 2008), p. 187.

"allowing children . . . speech in school"—William J. Faulkner, *The Days When the Animals Talked: Black American Folktales and How They Came To Be* (Trenton, NJ: Africa World Press, 1993), p. 7.

"All this has led to a rewrite . . ."—Lester, *Uncle Remus,* p. *x.*

PAGE 70 • "If that's the problem . . ."—Brasch, *Brer Rabbit,* p. 292, p. 122.

PAGE 71 • "even the bare suggestion . . . is unsavory"—R. Bruce Bickley, Jr., *Joel Chandler Harris* (Athens: University of Georgia Press, 1978), p. 36.

"an engaging but ignorant . . . black man"—Faulkner, *Days When the Animals Talked,* p. 8.

"I notices dat dem folks . . . come up"—Joel Chandler Harris, "How Mr. Rabbit Lost His Fine Bushy Tail" in *The Complete Tales of Uncle Remus* (Richard Chase comp.) (Boston: Houghton Mifflin, 1983), p. 75.

"Knowledge, opinion . . . gesture"—Ludwig Wittgenstein, *Remarks on the Philosophy of Psychology*, VOL. I, §928.

"taught him about life . . ."—Albert Murray, *South to a Very Old Place* (New York: Vintage Books, 1971), pp. 63–4.

PAGE 72 • "legendary tale of [their] race"—Paul M. Cousins, *Joel Chandler Harris: A Biography* (Baton Rouge, LA: Louisiana State University Press, 1968), p. 26.

"especially when he was . . . homesick"—Joel Chandler Harris, *On the Plantation: A Story of a Georgia Boy's Adventures during the War* (Athens, GA: University of Georgia Press, 1980), p. 105.

"breaking out in a torrent . . . heaven"—Lawrence W. Levine, *Black Culture and Black Consciousness: Afro-American Folk Thought from Slavery to Freedom* (Oxford: Oxford University Press, 2007), p. 21.

"sat next to one of the liveliest talkers . . . 'im room!'"—Joel Chandler Harris, *Nights with Uncle Remus: Myths and Legends of the Old Plantation* (John T. Bickley and R. Bruce Bickley, Jr. eds) (New York: Penguin Books, 2003), p. 10.

PAGE 72 • "*think* in the negro dialect"—Brasch, *Brer Rabbit*, p. 79.

PAGE 73 • "became an 'other fellow'"—Robert Cochran, "Black Father: The Subversive Achievement of Joel Chandler Harris," *African American Review* 38(4) (Spring 2004): 21–34.

"an identity which dogged him . . ."—Bickley, *Joel Chandler Harris*, p. 61.

"We simply cannot get beyond . . . today"—Brasch, *Brer Rabbit*, p. 300.

"the inner characteristic . . . native tongue it is"—James Whitcomb Riley, "Dialect," *Forum* (December 1893): 466; as cited in Brasch, *Brer Rabbit*, p. 150.

PAGE 74 • "des ez big ez life . . . nat'al"—Harris, "Aunt Tempy's Story" in *Complete Tales*, p. 277.

"He des lay dar . . . de sunshine"—Joel Chandler Harris, "A Story of a Blind Horse" in *Uncle Remus and His Friends: Old Plantation Stories, Songs, and Ballads with Sketches of Negro Characters* (Boston: Houghton Mifflin, 1892), p. 247.

"You marry en . . . got in it", "W'en in he prime/He tuck he time"—Harris, "Brother Rabbit Rescues Brother Terrapin" and "The Pimmerly Plum" in *Complete Tales*, p. 260, p. 372.

"[D]ialect . . . pronounced a failure"—Stella Brewer Brookes, *Joel Chandler Harris: Folklorist* (Athens: University of Georgia Press, 1972), pp. 117–18.

"The question whether . . . the experience"—Wittgenstein, *Remarks on the Philosophy of Psychology*, VOL. I, §20.

PAGE 75 • "The Dixie Pike . . . path in Africa"—Jean Toomer, *Cane* (New York: Harper & Row, 1969), p. 18.

"dark Victorian mausoleum complete with aspidistras"—Lane, *Tale of Beatrix Potter*, p. 34.

"I always thought . . . my parents"—Lear, *Beatrix Potter*, p. 66.

PAGES 76 • "Inside this cloistered existence . . ."—Lane, *Tale of Beatrix Potter*, pp. 30–1.

PAGE 77 • "but was generally stretched . . . hearth rug"—Lane, *Tale of Beatrix Potter*, p. 76.

PAGE 78 • "the peaceful time of childhood"—*Beatrix Potter: A Journal* (London: Penguin Books, 2006), np.

"so small . . . little mice", "My usual way of writing . . . the better"—Lane, *Tale of Beatrix Potter*, p. 49, p. 135.

"We don't see . . . beams, coruscates"—Wittgenstein, *Remarks on the Philosophy of Psychology*, VOL. I, §1100.

PAGE 78 • "the searching, expressionless stare of a little animal"—Lane, *Tale of Beatrix Potter*, p. 157.

PAGE 79 • "How awful . . . bitter fruit", "the enemy"—Lear, *Beatrix Potter*, p. 70, p. 94.

PAGE 80 • "I have been laughed at . . . child", "child in me . . . until I was fifty"—Lane, *Tale of Beatrix Potter*, p. 31, p. 59.

NOTES

PAGE 81 • "That picture . . . has done", "bold and firm . . . *hands move*", "I *will* do . . . later"—Beatrix Potter, *The Journal of Beatrix Potter: From 1881 to 1897* (transcribed by Leslie Linder) (London: Frederick Warne, 1966), p. 27, p. 28, p. 30.

PAGE 82 • "the irresistible desire . . . brought me round"—Lane, *Tale of Beatrix Potter*, p. 52.

PAGE 83 • "I can manage . . . rabbits"—Lane, *Tale of Beatrix Potter*, p. 138.

PAGE 84 • "Now of all the hopeless . . . fungus"—Lear, *Beatrix Potter*, p. 76.

"all the little tiny . . . story of life", "he became quite excited . . . colours"—*Journal of Beatrix Potter*, pp. 422–3, 298–9.

PAGE 86 • "de clock wuz . . . a-splutterin"—Harris, "Why Brer Wolf Didn't Eat the Little Rabbits" in *Complete Tales,* p. 468.

"The autumn is . . . pleasant", "in humble imitation . . . Fanny Burney"—*Journal of Beatrix Potter*, p. 351, p. 202.

"that makes the troubled spirits . . . go away"—Ishmael Reed, *Mumbo Jumbo* (New York: Scribner, 1996), p. 7.

"*absit omen*", "pique . . . amount of £6"—*Journal of Beatrix Potter*, pp. 203–4.

PAGE 88 • "My first act . . .", "I just had enough sense . . . lock him up"—*Journal of Beatrix Potter*, p. 205, p. 300.

PAGE 89 • "who had the power . . . potion or poison"—Eric J. Sundquist, *To Wake the Nations: Race in the Making in American Literature* (Cambridge, MA: Harvard University Press, 1993), pp. 366–7.

PAGE 91 • "men (spirits) . . . everyone knows this"—Wittgenstein, *Remarks on Frazer's* Golden Bough, p. 6.

PAGE 92 • "I read a story . . . of all hares", "proved scared . . . the family"—*Journal of Beatrix Potter*, p. 248, p. 239.

PAGE 93 • "I lay yo' ma got company . . . dat changes marters"—Harris, "Mr. Wolf Makes a Failure" in *Complete Tales,* p. 34.

"marks the first time . . . in her life"—John Goldthwaite, *The Natural History of Make-Believe: A Guide to the Principal Works of Britain, Europe, and America* (New York: Oxford University Press, 1996), p. 304.

PAGE 93 • "Uncle Remus consistently claims . . ."—Wayne Mixon, "The Ultimate Irrelevance of Race: Joel Chandler Harris and Uncle Remus in Their Time"; as cited in Brasch, *Brer Rabbit*, p. 77.

PAGE 94 • "I don't know . . . Cottontail and Peter", "She had been writing letters . . ."—Lear, *Beatrix Potter*, p. 86, p. 132.

"easy with itself . . . information of interest"—Goldthwaite, *Natural History of Make-Believe*, p. 313.

CHAPTER VII. OBLITERATURE

PAGE 97 • "Do you know who you are? . . ."—Henry James, *The Turn of the Screw* (New York: W.W. Norton, 1999), pp. 16; all subsequent quotations are from the same edition, pp. 124, 37, 127.

PAGE 98 • "Damned spirits all . . . oft made sport"—William Shakespeare, *A Midsummer Night's Dream*, III.2.

"a sort of sense of looking"—James, *Turn of the Screw*, p. 23.

PAGE 99 • "Gentles, perchance . . . let no man wonder"—Shakespeare, *Midsummer Night's Dream*, V.1.

"The children in special . . . save", "I was a screen . . . they would", "I was like a gaoler . . . escapes"—James, *Turn of the Screw*, pp. 25, 27, 53.

"Love looks not with the eyes . . . painted blind"—Shakespeare, *Midsummer Night's Dream*, I.1.

PAGE 100 • "What validates Dorn's lyric . . . unpredictably"—Tom Clark, *Edward Dorn: A World of Difference* (Berkeley, CA: North Atlantic Books, 2002), p. 14.

"scant enough 'antecedents'"—James, *Turn of the Screw*, p. 19.

"It would take another turn of the screw to desert"—Henry James, *What Maisie Knew* (New York: Penguin Books, 1985), p. 77.

"reason and love . . . together nowadays"—Shakespeare, *Midsummer Night's Dream*, III.1.

PAGE 101 • "up all night . . . sixteen-year-old girl"—Molly Haskell, *Frankly, My Dear*: Gone with the Wind *Revisited* (New Haven, CT: Yale University Press, 2009), p. 14.

"if you are an isolated captive . . ."—Judith Lewis Herman, MD, *Trauma and Recovery* (New York: Basic Books, 1992), p. 75.

PAGE 102 • "predator who marries three men she doesn't love"—Haskell, *Frankly, My Dear*, p.95.

"She found a way . . ."—Menza, Unpublished Work, pp. 65, 37, 43 .

"Ah, Scarlett, how the thought . . . sparkle"—Margaret Mitchell, *Gone with the Wind* (New York: Pocket Books, 2008), p. 929.

PAGE 103 • "I can't think about that now . . . tomorrow"—James Baldwin, *The Evidence of Things Not Seen* (New York: Henry Holt, 1985), p. *xvi*.

"She responded . . ."—Menza, Unpublished Work, pp. 121, 115.

PAGE 104 • "I read the entirety . . ."—Mitchell, *Gone with the Wind*, pp. 592, 878, 1070, 1035.

"was sentenced to death . . . 'Kill the Jew!'"—Charles Rutheiser, *Imagineering Atlanta: The Politics of Place in the City of Dreams* (London: Verso, 1996), p. 34.

"At Smith [College] . . . present"—Haskell, *Frankly, My Dear*, p. 200.

PAGE 105 • "dressed up like 'ghosts' . . ."—Mitchell, *Gone with the Wind*, p. 782.

"battalion of matrons . . . all of us"—Haskell, *Frankly, My Dear*, p. 147.

"Atlanta debutantes . . . the ball"—Rutheiser, *Imagineering Atlanta*, p. 43.

"the sixty-voice Ebenezer Baptist . . . dressed as slaves"—Brad Gooch, *Flannery: A Life of Flannery O'Connor* (New York: Little Brown, 2009), p. 68.

"There were dozens . . .", "In 1932 . . . Uncle Remus characters"—Brasch, *Brer Rabbit*, p. 285n2, pp. 271–2.

"could hardly explain . . . demonically onward"—Haskell, *Frankly, My Dear*, p. 95.

PAGE 106 • "'Fast' was the only word for Scarlett"—Mitchell, *Gone with the Wind*, p. 144.

"partial psychopath"—Hervy Cleckley, M.D., *The Mask of Sanity: An Attempt to Clarify Some Issues About the So-Called Psychopathic Personality*, 5TH EDN (St. Louis, MO: C.V. Mosby, 1976), p. 89.

"hunted as a fox," "Even though"—Mitchell, *Gone with the Wind,* pp. 848–9.

"Accept the first hint of a hitching tiller"—Herman Melville, *Moby Dick* (New York: Modern Library, 1992), p. 611.

"They haven't any more spirit than a rabbit . . ."—Mitchell, *Gone with the Wind,* p. 107, p. 68, p. 323, p. 851, p. 678, p. 917, p. 1169.

PAGE 107 • "And I sweat blood . . ."—Richard Harwell (ed.), *Margaret Mitchell's "Gone with the Wind" Letters, 1936–1949* (New York: Macmillan, 1976), pp. 32–3.

"I think Margie's reading . . . dissolved"—Herman, *Trauma and Recovery,* p. 81.

PAGE 108 • "is the active exercise . . . and happy"—Aristotle, *The Nicomachean Ethics*, 1098a17–21.

PAGE 109 • "the main idea . . . ", "happiness is self-contained"—John Rawls, *A Theory of Justice*, REV. EDN (Cambridge, MA: Harvard University Press, 1999[1971]), pp. 79–80, 481.

"carries from the beginning . . . *career*"—Gerald F. Else, *Aristotle's Poetics*: *The Argument* (Cambridge, MA: Harvard University Press, 1963), p. 257.

"Skeat derives 'career'"—Rev. Walter W. Skeat, *An Etymological Dictionary of the English Language* (Oxford: Oxford University Press, 1963), p. 92.

"No one allows a slave . . . of his own"—Aristotle, *Nicomachean Ethics,* 1177a8–9.

PAGE 110 • "Only the intended picture . . . with real things"—Ludwig Wittgenstein, *Zettel* (G. E. M. Anscombe and G. H. von Wright eds, G. E. M. Anscombe trans.) (Berkeley: University of California Press, 1967), p. 233.

PAGE 111 • "if you do not love life . . ."—Leo Tolstoy, *The Gospel in Brief* (Isabel Hapgood trans.) (New York: Dover Publications, 2008), p. 134.

"Aristotle came from a culture . . ."—Else, *Aristotle's Poetics,* p. 77.

"Rawls had an attenuated concept of the person . . ."—John Rawls, *Justice as Fairness: A Restatement* (Erin Kelly ed.) (Cambridge, MA: Harvard University Press, 2003), pp. 18–19, 24.

"Joy is represented . . . it exists"—Wittgenstein, *Remarks on the Philosophy of Psychology*, VOL. I, §853.

PAGE 112 • "Do not lay up for yourselves . . . light"—Matthew 6.19, 6.21–2.

"Each person we walked past . . . other's names"—Brice O'Connell, "An Unforgettable Experience," *Action on Colombia* [Colombia Support Network Newsletter] (Summer 2012): 3–4.

PAGE 113 • "They have found the Occupy Movement"—Naomi Klein, "Occupy Wall Street: The Most Important Thing in the World Now," *The Nation* (October 6, 2011).

"Fine shades of behavior . . . consequences"—Wittgenstein, *Philosophical Investigations,* §240.

CHAPTER VIII. HOW CHILDREN GET CHEATED OUT OF THEIR HUMANITY

PAGE 114 • "Hence Dilthey saw scientific knowledge . . . with life"—Hans-Georg Gadamer, *Truth and Method* (New York: Continuum, 1975), p. 8. Originally published as *Wahrheit und Methode* by J. C. B. Mohr [Paul Siebeck] in 1960.

PAGE 115 • "Children are persistently misunderstood . . . leverage"—Brasch, *Brer Rabbit,* p. 173.

"She has the wonderful importance . . ."—James, *What Maisie Knew,* p. 29.

PAGE 116 • "Sheer humanity radiates forth . . ."—Tom Roeper, *The Prism of Grammar: How Child Language Illuminates Humanism* (Cambridge, MA: MIT Press, 2007), pp. 45–6.

"With no banal reassuring grown-ups . . ."—Elizabeth Bowen, *The House in Paris* (New York: Anchor Books, 2002), p. 20.

PAGE 117 • "For nobody to whom life . . ."—James, *What Maisie Knew,* p. 31.

PAGE 118 • "It was uncanny . . ."—Paul Bloom, *How Children Lean the Meanings of Words* (Cambridge, MA: MIT Press, 2001), p. 134.

PAGE 119 • "I am I because my little dog knows me"—Gertrude Stein, *The Geographical History of America* (New York: Random House, 1973), *passim.*

PAGE 122 • "I am listening to a girl"—D. W. Winnicott, *Playing and Reality* (New York: Brunner-Routledge, 2002), p. 73.

PAGE 125 • "A child's everyday concept . . . an abstract one"—Lev Vygotsky, *Thought and Language* (Alex Kozulin trans.) (Cambridge, MA: MIT Press, 1986), pp. 192–3.

PAGE 126 • "It is not possible for a child . . . interpretation"—D. W. Winnicott, *The Piggle*: *An Account of the Psychoanalytic Treatment of a Little Girl* (Ishak Ramzy ed.) (Madison, CT: International Universities Press, 1977), p. 175.

"She was at the age . . . vivid"—James, *What Maisie Knew,* p. 42.

PAGE 127 • "There is a juncture . . ."—A. R. Luria, *Cognitive Development*: *Its Cultural and Social Foundations* (Michael Cole ed., Martin Lopez-Morillas and Lynn Solotaroff trans) (Cambridge, MA: Harvard University Press, 1976), p. 85.

"systematic reasoning in connection with concepts . . ."—Vygotsky, *Thought and Language,* p. 174.

PAGE 128 • "The egg-shell of its origin . . . break free"—Wittgenstein, *Remarks on the Philosophy of Psychology*, VOL. I, §1124.

CHAPTER IX. THE RABBIT BETWEEN US CAME FROM SLAVERY

PAGE 130 • "Slavery was not born of racism . . . slavery"—Eric Williams, *Capitalism and Slavery* (Chapel Hill: University of North Carolina Press, 1994), p. 7; as cited in Susan Buck-Morss, *Hegel, Haiti, and Universal History* (Pittsburgh, PA: University of Pittsburgh Press, 2009).

"A tribe that we want to enslave . . . purpose whatever"—Wittgenstein, *Remarks on the Philosophy of Psychology*, VOL. I, §96.

PAGE 131 • "that nothing is more human . . . in particular cases"—Mulhall, *Philosophical Myths of the Fall,* p. 94.

"The reality of slave existence . . . death"—James H. Cone, *The Spirituals and the Blues*: *An Interpretation* (Maryknoll, NY: Seabury Press, 1972), p. 27.

"Yet slavery had always been . . . burdens of history"—David Brion Davis, *The Problem of Slavery in Western Culture* (Ithaca, NY: Cornell University Press, 1966), p. 10.

PAGE 132 • "The United States imprisons . . . of apartheid"—Michelle Alexander, *The New Jim Crow: Mass Incarceration in the Age of Colorblindness*, REV. EDN (New York: New Press, 2012[2010]), p. 6.

"Again and again the assumption . . . less American"—Albert Murray, *The Omni-Americans: Some Alternatives to the Folklore of White Supremacy* (New York: Outerbridge & Dienstrey, 1970), p. 36.

"Ain't no justice, It's just us"—D'Angelo and DJ Premier, "Devil's Pie" in *Voodoo* (Virgin Records, 2000).

"Orlando Patterson divides slavery . . . "—Orlando Patterson, *Slavery and Social Death: A Comparative Study* (Cambridge, MA: Harvard University Press, 1982), pp. 5–10.

PAGES 132–3 • "Honor consisteth only in the opinion of power"—Thomas Hobbes, *Leviathan* (Cambridge: Cambridge University Press, 1904), p. 59.

PAGE 133 • "a person's honor . . . mind"—Patterson, *Slavery and Social Death*, p. 78.

"He, having the divine nature . . . man"—Garry Wills, *What Jesus Meant* (New York: Penguin Books, 2006), p. *xxviii*; Philippians, 2.6–11.

"He is never concerned with upholding his own honor"—Guardini, *The Humanity of Christ*, p. 99.

"most slaves did not succumb . . . suicide"—Eugene D. Genovese, *Roll, Jordan, Roll: The World the Slaves Made* (New York: Vintage Books, 1976), pp. 638–40.

"A communalism born of oppression . . . life "—John W. Blassingame, *The Slave Community: Plantation Life in the Antebellum South*, REV. EDN (New York: Oxford University Press, 1979[1972]), p. 148.

PAGE 134 • "inverted totalitarianism"—Sheldon S. Wolin, *Democracy Incorporated: Managed Democracy and the Specter of Inverted Totalitarianism* (Princeton, NJ: Princeton University Press, 2008), p. 57.

PAGE 135 • "Dat de reason I don't . . . sayin it"—Harris, "Brother Rabbit's Laughing-Place" in *Complete Tales*, p. 567.

PAGE 136 • "that fox"—Luke 13:31–32.

"The Holy Spirit descends . . ."—Mark 1:11.

"How often would I have . . . you would not"—Matthew 23:37.

"Behold, the Lamb . . . the world"—John 1:29.

"It is literally true . . . such a gadfly"—Plato, *Apology,* 30E.

"the route by which the fable . . . Socratic dialogue"—F. R. Adrados, *History of the Graeco-Latin Fable,* VOL. 1; as cited in Leslie Kurke, *Aesopic Conversations: Popular Tradition, Cultural Dialogue, and the Invention of Greek Prose* (Princeton, NJ: Princeton University Press, 2011), p. 269.

PAGE 137 • "I am sure that if Aesop . . . that follows it"—Plato, *Phaedo,* 60C.

"Socrates in Xenophon's *Memorabilia* . . . when animals could talk"—Xenophon, *Conversations of Socrates* (Robin Waterfield ed. and trans., Hugh Tredennick trans.) (London: Penguin Books, 1990), II.vii.13.

"Socrates tells the fable of the cicadas"—Plato, *Phaedrus,* 258E–259D.

"I think, gentlemen, that men's poverty . . . souls"—Donald R. Dudley, *A History of Cynicism from Diogenes to the Sixth Century AD* (London: Bristol Classical Press, 2003), p. 8.

"snails and wingless locusts"—Diogenes Laertius, *Lives of Eminent Philosophers,* 2 VOLS (R. D. Hicks trans.) (Cambridge, MA: Harvard University Press, 1972), VI.1–2.

PAGE 138 • "Honey, you look so much . . . run or no"—Harris, "The Reason Why" in *Complete Tales,* p. 544.

"The only difference . . . slaves"—Plato, *Symposium,* 215C–E.

PAGE 139 • "began to sing about . . . a *prisoner*"—Harris, "Why Mr. Cricket has Elbows on His Legs" in *Complete Tales,* p. 549; emphasis added.

"the first to deplore the system . . . little fellow"—Harris, "The Hard-Headed Woman" in *Complete Tales,* p. 666.

"With lamentably few exceptions . . ."—June Jordan, "A Truly Bad Rabbit," *The New York Times* (May 17, 1987).

PAGE 140 • "He got a mighty quick eye . . . mighty still"—Harris, "'Heyo, House!'" in *Complete Tales,* 516.

"The joint knowledge of the tales . . ."—Levine, *Black Culture*, p. 97.

"You er one er deze . . . you is"—Harris, "Brother Rabbit Has Fun at the Ferry" in *Complete Tales*, p. 462.

"de snow on de grave crack . . . bury him"—Sterling Stuckey, *Slave Culture: Nationalist Theory and the Foundations of Black America* (New York: Oxford University Press, 1987), p. 19.

"Brer Rabbit's victories . . . itself"—Levine, *Black Culture*, p. 113.

"slave consciousness . . . faith"—Stuckey, *Slave Culture*, p. 30.

"They both have protuberant eyes . . .", "the power-to-make-things-happen . . ."—Robert Farris Thompson, *Flash of the Spirit: African & Afro-American Art & Philosophy* (New York: Vintage Books, 1984), p. 28, p. 5.

PAGE 141 • "translation of *àshe* as *logos* . . ."—Henry Louis Gates, Jr., *The Signifying Monkey: A Theory of African-American Literary Criticism* (Oxford: Oxford University Press, 1988), p. 7.

"Brer Rabbit wuz de soopless [supplest] creetur gwine"—Harris, "Brother Rabbit's Astonishing Prank" in *Complete Tales*, p. 124.

"The word came from the French *soupple*"—Skeat, *An Etymological Dictionary of the English Language*, p. 531.

"Beware! Don't celebrate this fickle . . . you're free"—Jalaloddin Rumi, *Spiritual Verses: The First Book of the Masnavi-ye Ma'navi* (Alan Williams trans.) (New York: Penguin Books, 2006), line 1378.

PAGE 143 • "Listen to this reed . . . see the soul"—Rumi, *Spiritual Verses,* lines 1, 5, 6, 8.

"It is, in short, pointless . . . one's own"—Jean-Jacques Rousseau, *Confessions*, Book II (Angela Scholar trans.) (Oxford: Oxford University Press, 2000), p. 80.

"great as is the charm . . . varied"—W. A. Bentley and George H. Perkins, "A Study of Snow Crystals," *Popular Science Monthly* 53 (May 1898): 77, 81.

CHAPTER X. AUBADE WITH BRER RABBIT

PAGE 145 • "The question 'Real or not?'. . . they seem"—J. L. Austin, *Sense and Sensibilia*, reconstructed from the manuscript notes by G. J. Warnock

(Oxford: Oxford University Press, 1962), p. 69; all subsequent quotations are from the same edition; p. 64, p. 70.

"I dunner what would a happen . . . bag anymo'"—Harris, "How Riley Wolf Rode in the Bag" in *Complete Tales,* p. 562.

PAGE 146 • "Real isn't how you are made . . . you"—Margery Williams, *The Velveteen Rabbit, or How Toys Become Real* (New York: Doubleday, 1991), p. 5.

"the body remains . . . the soul's necessary covering"—Romano Guardini, *The Lord* (Elinor C. Briefs trans.) (Washington, DC: Gateway Editions, 1996), p. 274.

"the human body is the best picture of the human soul"—Ludwig Wittgenstein, *Philosophical Investigations,* REV. 4TH EDN (P. M. S. Hacker and Joachim Schulte eds) (G. E. M. Anscombe, P. M. S. Hacker, and Joachim Schulte trans) (Oxford: Wiley-Blackwell, 2009), Part II, pp. *iv;* 25 [unnumbered in earlier editions].

"male, mobile, master of language . . . light"—Ruth Padel, *In and Out of Mind: Greek Images of the Tragic Self* (Princeton, NJ: Princeton University Press, 1992), p. 6.

PAGE 147 • "not allowed to stay . . . League of Atlanta"—Brasch, *Brer Rabbit,* p. 279, p. 281.

"Aunt Tempy? . . ."—Walt Disney (producer), *Song of the South* (RKO Radio Pictures, 1946).

PAGE 149 • "And just like I told him . . ."—Disney, *Song of the South.*

PAGE 150 • "why she started illustrating tales . . ."—Goldthwaite, *Natural History of Make-Believe,* p. 304.

"an audience made up largely of happy, responding kids"—Brasch, *Brer Rabbit,* p. 282.

PAGE 151 • "Cab Calloway"—Ishmael Reed, *Cab Calloway Stands In for the Moon* (Flint, MI: Bamberger Books, 1986).

PAGE 152 • "protective societies gave annual balls . . ."—John F. Szwed, *Space Is the Place: The Lives and Times of Sun Ra* (Cambridge, MA: Da Capo Press, 1998), pp. 14–15.

"Mr. Bluebird on her shoulder . . . satisfactual"—"Zip-a-Dee-Doo-Dah" per-fomed by James Baskett in the film *Song of the South*.

PAGE 154 • "Having reseen *Song of the South* . . ."—Thomas Metzinger, *Being No One: The Self-Model Theory of Subjectivity* (Cambridge, MA: MIT Press, 2003), p. 239.

PAGE 155 • "Everybody who has had . . . certain renunciations"—Victor Hugo, *Les Misérables* (Charles E. Wilbour trans.) (New York: Alfred A. Knopf, 1997[1909]), p. 1324.

CHAPTER XI. THE RABBIT DANCES

PAGE 157 • "Also the classical theory of art . . . contained in imitation"—Gadamer, *Truth and Method*, p. 102.

PAGE 158 • "Make a bow ter de Buzzard . . . Jim Crow"—Joel Chandler Harris, "How Mr. Rabbit Succeeded in Raising a Dust" in *Uncle Remus: His Songs and His Sayings*, REV. EDN (New York: Hawthorne Books, 1921), p. 150.

"We played the pipes . . . We sang a dirge . . ."—Burton L. Mack, *The Lost Gospel: The Book of Q and Christian Origins* (New York: HarperCollins, 1993), p. 86.

"Hate between men . . . each other"—Ludwig Wittgenstein, *Culture and Value* (G. H. von Wright ed., Peter Winch trans.) (Chicago: University of Chicago Press, 1980), p. 46.

"When the Muses . . . noticing it"—Plato, *Phaedrus*, 259BC.

PAGE 159 • "reveal the *psyche* . . . engage with you"—James Davidson, *The Greeks and Greek Love* (New York: Random House, 2009), p. 45.

"Feelings accompany . . . our life"—Wittgenstein, *Culture and Value*, p. 10.

"Blacks were able . . . had already come"—Cone, *The Spirituals and the Blues*, p. 86.

"Music is something which . . . adds to us"—John Miller Chernoff, *African Rhythm and African Sensibility: Aesthetics and Social Action in African Musical Idioms* (Chicago: University of Chicago Press, 1979), p. 35.

"Music makes the internal external . . ."—Wynton Marsalis, with Geoffrey C. Ward, *Moving to Higher Ground: How Jazz Can Change Your Life* (New York: Random House, 2008), p. 76, p. 80.

PAGE 160 • "The seventeenth-century French philosopher . . ."—René Descartes, *Discourse on Method,* Part II (1637) quoted in Robert Audi (ed.), *The Cambridge Dictionary of Philosophy* (Cambridge: Cambridge University Press, 1995), p. 193.

"I look out the window . . .", "I might consider . . ."—René Descartes, *Meditations,* II, from *The Philosophical Writings of Descartes,* VOL. II (John Cottingham, Robert Stoothoff, and Dugald Murdoch trans) (Cambridge: Cambridge University Press, 2007), p. 21, p. 58.

PAGE 161 • "nasty belch", "the slave is recognized . . ."—Joan Dayan, *Haiti, History, and the Gods* (Berkeley: University of California Press, 1998), p. 204, p. 205.

"Nor can anyone know . . . 'wrong' use"—Wittgenstein, *Philosophical Investigations,* §§243–58; as cited in Anthony Kenny, *Action, Emotion, and Will,* 2ND EDN (London: Routledge, 2003[1963]), p. 9.

"I feel the other . . . therefore I am"—Léopold Sédar Senghor, *Négritude et humanisme, Liberté,* VOL. 1 (Paris: Seuil, 1964).

PAGE 162 •"Human beings are made for each other . . . for others"—James H. Cone, *God of the Oppressed,* REV. EDN (Maryknoll, NY: Orbis Books, 1997), p. *xiii.*

LIST OF ILLUSTRATIONS

FRONTISPIECE • Michael Sowa, *Im Zug* (acrylic on paper, 1993). Reproduced with kind permission of the artist.

PAGE 13 • Victoria Blewer, *Here It Is* (hand-colored photograph, 1991). Reproduced with the kind permission of the artist.

PAGE 18 • J. M. W. Turner, *Rain, Steam and Speed* (oil on canvas, 1844, National Gallery, London). This image is now in the public domain, and is available at Wikimedia Commons.

PAGE 63 • Titian, *The Madonna of the Rabbit* (oil on canvas, *c.* 1530, Louvre Museum, Paris). This image is now in the public domain, and is available at Wikimedia Commons.

PAGE 131 • Illustration by Arthur Burdett Frost (1896) in Joel Chandler Harris, "Mr. Rabbit and Mr. Bear". This image is in the public domain, and is available at Internet Archive.

PAGE 154 • A photograph from the author's personal collection.

PAGE 158 • Illustration by Arthur Burdett Frost (1896) in Joel Chandler Harris, "How Mr. Rabbit Succeeded in Raising a Dust". This image is in the public domain, and is available at Internet Archive.